Acknowledgments

This book would not have become a reality without the support of many dear friends in Churchill, Manitoba. I would like to express my thanks and gratitude to the following people:

My wife Eleonore, who has shown patience, tolerance and understanding for my work and is an active partner in all my projects.

Richard and Julia Jean, the operators of Kelsey Lodge, who provided Eleonore and me with a place to stay for an extended period of time and made us feel like members of the family.

Brian Ladoon, dog breeder, sled guide, trapper, fisherman and painter, a friend who "fathered" several of my pictures.

Luise Foubert, Dwight Allen and Dan Foubert, managers of the Polar Inn, who made me feel at home after Kelsey Lodge closed.

Joan Schweder, who actively supported my photographic efforts in all weather conditions.

Dennis Andriashek and Dr. Ian Sterling from the Canadian Wildlife Service, who provided invaluable assistance in the polar bear cubs' story. Thanks again for your wonderful cooperation.

Steve "The Eagle" Miller, master helicopter pilot in the arctic air.

Elisabeth and Bill Calnan, who frequently invited me to their home in Goose Creek to warm up during the frosty polar nights when I was shooting the northern lights.

Guy and Bill Alikut and Donald Uluadluak, who were my summertime guides for the story on arctic foxes.

Mike Macri from Seg North Tours, who escorted me on boat trips to see the whales and the icebergs.

Edgar Bothelho, a partner and friend.

Thanks also to: Donnie Walkosky and family; Penny Rawlings and the people at the Arctic Trading Post; Lynn Rollin from Arviat; Manuel Duarte and family of Gypsy's Bakery; Lorraine Brandson from the Eskimo Museum; Jouliette and Lindy Lee; Mike Lawson and Paula; Bob Taylor, Mike Reimer and the team of Northwind Auto; Bruce Marten, Wayne Bilenduke, Allen Code and family; Dale Cook and Edward Zipf from the NASA Team 1989; Bill and Diane Erickson from Boreal Garden; Bonnie Chartier from Wilderness Encounter; Dan Guravich, Len and Beth Smith from Tundra Buggy Tours; Walter Picket and employees of Parks Canada; and many other helping hands in Churchill.

The pilots of Keewatin Air, Calm Air and Canadian Airlines International, St. Regis Hotel/Winnipeg.

Hubert and Brigitte Tecklenborg and Jan Tölle, who were instrumental in the production of this book.

Special thanks to Fritz Pölking for his many ideas and friendly support.

Thanks for technical support and consultation go to LEICA Camera GmbH, Solms, Munich, and ISAR Foto Klaus Bothe, Icking.

Assistance for original text (in German) and editing: Eleonore Rosing, Wolfgang Alexander Bajohr, Dr. Fritz Jantschke, Luidger Weyers, Felix Knauer and Ulrich Wotschikowsky from the Wild Biologic Association Munich e.V.

Translation was done by Max Basting, Fr.-Ebert-Ring 218, D-48429 Rheine, Germany. Contact: Tecklenborg Verlag or Norbert Rosing.

The sun, the symbol of life and the sign of a new day.
Photograph taken from 33,000 feet.

For Father

The World of the
Polar Bear

Norbert Rosing

FIREFLY BOOKS

A Firefly Book

Published by Firefly Books Ltd.
1996

First published in German as
Im Reich des Polarbären in 1994
by Tecklenborg Verlag

Cataloguing-in-Publication Data

Rosing, Norbert
  The world of the polar bear

Translation of: Im Reich des
Polarbären.
ISBN 1-55209-068-X

1. Polar bears.   I. Title.

QL737.C27R6613   1996
599.74'446   C96-930595-8

Published by
Firefly Books Ltd.
3680 Victoria Park Avenue
Willowdale, Ontario
Canada M2H 3K1

Published in the U.S. by
Firefly Books (U.S.) Inc.
P.O. Box 1338, Ellicott Station
Buffalo, New York 14205

Printed in Canada by Friesens
Altona, Manitoba

Printed on acid-free paper

Contents

*Wildlife researcher **Dr. Ian Stirling** has studied polar bear behavior for more than 25 years. A research scientist with the Canadian Wildlife Service, Stirling is also an adjunct professor of zoology at the University of Alberta, in Edmonton. He has published three books on polar bears and has written more than 100 scientific articles about polar bears, seals and arctic marine ecology.*

Surrounded by glistening ice crystals, a polar bear rests in the late afternoon's red light.

Introduction

The polar bear is an animal that needs no introduction: it is one of the most recognized animals in the world. At the same time, there is so much that most people don't know about the polar bear in its home, the circumpolar Arctic. Nanook, its Inuit name, is both familiar and a mystery to us.

When, in the 1960s, there was worldwide public concern that the polar bear would become endangered because of rapidly increasing levels of harvest, the five "polar bear nations"—Canada, Denmark, Norway, the former U.S.S.R. and the United States—responded. In 1973, they signed the International Agreement on the Conservation of Polar Bears and Their Habitat, in Oslo, Norway. This agreement required each country to manage polar bears according to sound conservation practices based on the best scientific information available, to conserve polar bear habitat and to maintain national research programs. For many years, the conservation of polar bears was the only subject in the entire Arctic that nations from both sides of the Iron Curtain could agree upon sufficiently to sign an agreement. Such was the intensity of human fascination with this magnificent predator, the only marine bear.

Now, after more than 20 years of intense research into the movements, population dynamics, behavior and general biology of the polar bear, it appears that populations are secure for the foreseeable future.

We have learned an incredible amount about how the polar bear has become so adapted to life in the Arctic. Even so, we are still humbled to realize how much we have yet to understand about the biology of polar bears.

Nevertheless, the polar bear remains the single most powerful symbol of the Arctic and represents the supreme adaptation to one of the world's harshest yet variable environments. The white bear has its own presence at many different levels, depending on whether the viewer is an Inuk hunter, a shaman, a scientist, a naturalist, a photographer, a poet or simply a casual observer. No one just walks past a polar bear, even if he or she has seen hundreds before; every single bear is special and worthy of special appreciation. In a nutshell, this book is important because it captures some of the essential spirit of the polar bear.

Many people visit the Arctic, and most enjoy the experience. Some go only to see a polar bear and are happy even if they sight only one. However, a few special people develop a deep love and understanding not only of the polar bear itself but of the essence of what it is and how it has become part of the environment. For them, it is not enough just to see a polar bear; they seek to understand the animal on its own terms, in the environment to which it has become so incredibly adapted.

Norbert Rosing is one of those who has been "bitten by the arctic bug" and has developed a special fascination with polar bears. Thus he has returned to Churchill for several years and in all seasons to photograph polar bears and their habitat. Fortunately for the reader, he is a gifted photographer. As a result of his patience and dedication, he has developed one of the most outstanding collections of polar bear photographs I have ever seen. However, of equal importance to me as a scientist, he has succeeded in capturing the essence of the habitat of polar bears in western Hudson Bay and of many of the other species that share its environment, such as the arctic fox. Another superbly adapted arctic mammal, the arctic fox has developed a special relationship with polar bears, often following the bears onto the sea ice through the winter and surviving by scavenging the remains of seals killed by the bears. The vastness of the sea ice habitat in which the polar bear is at home must be seen to be appreciated. To see a bear in subzero temperatures, mostly covered in snow and

A mother bear and her cubs seek shelter behind a wall of compacted snow during a blinding winter blizzard along the icy Hudson Bay coast.

sound asleep in a snowdrift, gives a momentary insight into how remarkably well the polar bear has adapted to its environment.

Through the photographs and writing in this book, you can sense many facets of the variable personalities of polar bears. Bears are, of course, powerful and impressive simply because of their physical presence. However, it may come as a delightful surprise to many readers to discover their intense curiosity, to see the clown that plays with an old tire, to sense the gentle and ever-caring mother and to wonder at the truly amazing photographs of a polar bear gently playing with a sled dog. Of course, the incredible diversity of behavior within the species, and in fact within each individual bear, is what makes polar bears so special and continuously interesting.

Despite all we have learned about polar bears in recent years, we cannot become too complacent. Humans and industrial development continue to encroach upon the Arctic, both directly and indirectly, through airborne pollutants and possible changes to the climate. All these factors may affect the future of polar bears. Even ecotourism can be harmful when polar bears are lured closer with food for photographs and lose their fear of humans. If we are to conserve polar bears and the Arctic for future generations, then we must learn about them; on their terms, not ours. This beautiful book will increase your understanding of polar bears and their habitat.

DR. IAN STIRLING

How It All Began…

Photo: Dennis Andriashek

The Dog Days of Summer
Unable to hunt seals, their favorite food, when Hudson Bay
is free of ice, polar bears spend the days from July until
November lounging around inland.

My arctic adventure began late one cold February afternoon in 1983 in a library in downtown Winnipeg, Manitoba. Just a few hours earlier, I had stepped off a Greyhound bus from Montreal. I had intended to spend the night in Winnipeg, then continue west on my Canadian odyssey to Whitehorse, in the Yukon Territory. My plans, however, were about to change drastically.

Stooped over the library's expansive maps of Hudson Bay and the arctic region, I was anticipating the adventure ahead when my reverie was interrupted by the voice of a young Inuk. "Planning a trip north?" he asked casually. When I nodded, he continued: "The arctic experience in winter is mostly about learning to love the cold. Luckily, you don't have to go all the way to Resolute Bay to find it. Just take the train north to Churchill, Manitoba. If it isn't cold enough for you there, I'd have to recommend a trip to the South Pole."

It was an intriguing idea. As it turned out, the stranger's advice was all the encouragement I needed to board the train for Churchill the next morning. The train proceeded at a moderate speed until we reached the mining town of Thompson. From there, we crawled at a snail's pace across what is known as the Muskeg Route. Occasionally, lights shone from the darkness as workers signaled the railroad men to clear snowdrifts from the tracks ahead or to heat the line switches to prevent derailment. I was almost at the end of my patience—having endured some 1,000 miles of a landscape that seemed like endless wheat belt and boreal forest—when we finally left the tree line behind. Roughly 36 hours into our trip, Churchill at last lay ahead.

The stretch of rail between the towns of The Pas and Churchill was first surveyed in 1911, and in a show of true pioneering spirit, it was ready for service by 1929. The connection was crucial for shipping grain from southern Manitoba and Saskatchewan to the storage elevators at Churchill, which was the only international harbor on Hudson Bay. A symbol of the town's historic importance as a trading center, Churchill's silos—which hold more than 100,000 tons of grain—have defined the local skyline since their completion in 1931.

The morning of my arrival, the weather was overcast and snowy. When a sudden storm transformed the town into an icy desert, I couldn't see a single car in the street or, for that matter, any other sign of human life. Was this the same majestic land of ice whose image I had so warmly savored in my imagination? Like a tortoise in its shell, I retreated deep into my parka, hoisted my heavy rucksack over my shoulder and fought my way toward the town's only open hotel, the

Tundra Inn, stumbling backward as I braced myself against the wind. Before I turned in for the night, I made a telephone call to my folks in Germany, hoping that their familiar voices would somehow alleviate my sense of disappointment and frustration.

At the reception desk the next morning, I was greeted by a young man with whom I was to form a lasting friendship. His name was Paul Ratson, and he generously offered to take me out on the tundra. Sweetening his offer, he also invited me to stay with him and his family at their home. With Paul's guidance, the next few days provided an eventful mix of new adventures, although each one was tinged by my arctic inexperience. For the first time in my life, for example, I saw a dazzling display of northern lights—the aurora borealis—but the bitterly cold temperatures prevented my capturing the show in pictures. Not only did my film freeze and break, but my camera stopped functioning for good.

When my two-day arctic sojourn was over, I was happy to leave Churchill and its inhospitable cold spell behind. As I sped away (this time on board an airplane), I had no idea that Churchill, Manitoba—the polar bear capital of the world—would one day become my home away from home.

The Polar Bear Bug

Since that trial-by-fire introduction to the Canadian North, I have grown from a novice hobbyist into an experienced professional nature and wildlife photographer. Today, I devote a good deal of my time to polar bears, actually enjoying the weeks that I spend studying them in their arctic habitat. Visiting the Hudson Bay region around Churchill as often as three times a year, I never miss the busy fall season when gangs of hungry polar bears make their annual pilgrimage to the small coastal town and take advantage of the region's early freeze-up to hunt for seals. It is a transient aggregation unprecedented in all the world.

Before I had seen *Ursus maritimus*, I had no idea what to expect. But from the instant I laid eyes on one of these regal creatures, I experienced a rush of adrenaline, a heady hybrid of respect and awe that has continued to fuel my passion for Nanook, the name given to him by the indigenous people of the Canadian Arctic. Holding the record as the world's largest terrestrial carnivore, the polar bear—also known as the King of the Arctic —can't help being impressive upon first sighting: females range in size from 330 to 770 pounds, while males weigh between 660 and 1,500 pounds. The tallest of the bunch stands 10 feet on its hind legs.

Scientists and researchers know the feeling well and say that this passion is the consequence of being bitten by the "polar bear bug." Like any other fever, the polar bear bug has a number of symptoms, not the least of which is simply admiration for the bears. Its lingering effect also includes a deeper appreciation for all northern regions, where one's mind is free to roam across an endless countryside whose lifeblood is contrast: raging snowstorms and sculptures of glistening ice; clear azure skies by day and ghostly northern lights by night; the setting of the radiant sun and the rising of the full moon. It awakens your senses to the richness inherent in an austere land, where the still, crisp air can be fractured by the haunting calls of cranes, auks and wild geese flying overhead or by the unrelenting whir of a common mosquito's wings buzzing about your head.

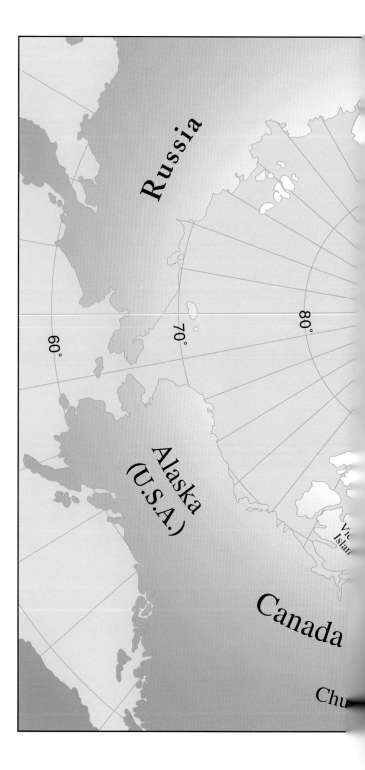

Scandinavia

60°

0°

90°

Ellesmere Island

Iceland

Greenland

Baffin Island

Shortly before the ice covers Hudson Bay in late fall, hundreds of polar bears return to the Churchill area and pass the time play-fighting.

13

14

Churchill, Manitoba
The Polar Bear Capital of the World

Churchill in summertime; Kelsey Boulevard is the town's main street.

*Facing page, clockwise from top left: An aerial view of
Churchill's harbor during the summer; a wintertime
view of Churchill's grain elevators, a prominent landmark;
the abandoned local military post and water tower;
Churchill's railroad station, the final stop of the "Muskeg
Express" from Winnipeg.*

Prior to the early 1980s, not many people were familiar with the town
of Churchill, Manitoba, aside from the farmers of the wheat-producing
prairies, who shipped their grain to the nearest harbor at Churchill Port,
and employees of Canadian National Railways, who rode the desolate
lines to this northern terminus.

Seven hundred miles by air from Winnipeg—the bustling capital of
Manitoba—Churchill is located at 58 degrees 44 minutes north latitude,
the same latitude as Stockholm, Sweden, and Oslo, Norway. The view
of the town from an airplane perfectly reveals its isolation, sitting right
in the middle of the endless Canadian tundra that skirts the true Arctic.
Four large but distinct habitats also meet in this area: the wide Churchill
River to the north, the salty waters of Hudson Bay to the east and the
tree line to the south and west. Like a pair of geographical bookends
bordering either side of the Churchill environment, the roots of the
boreal forest are buried deep in the cold soil immediately south of the
tree line and the arctic Barren Lands bear down from the north some
25 miles away.

The confluence of these four regions explains the wealth of natural
life in the Churchill area, which in turn explains its newfound fame. In
the short time since 1980, Churchill has become an internationally
renowned center for wildlife research and ecotourism, its name synony-
mous with polar bears, northern lights, massive bird migrations, whale
pods and a harsh landscape that manages to surprise visitors by yielding
colorful annual crops of wildflowers. Scientists, photographers and film
teams are among the 10,000 people who flock to the town each year.

While the never-ending activity of tourists and scientists creates a
tremendous transient population within this town, a harmonious mix of
aboriginal, Inuit and a handful of peoples of European descent make up
the permanent population of Churchill. Outnumbered by visitors approximately eight to one, local residents rely on their town's naturally
isolated setting to safeguard its unspoiled charm and character. Air and
rail travel offer the only access to the nearest larger communities, 100
miles away.

Churchill, Manitoba: A Historic Overview

1610: Henry Hudson discovers the strait from the ocean to the bay that was named after him.

1619: Jens Munck, a Dane, discovers the mouth of the Churchill River. Only Munck and two of his comrades survive the harsh winter; all other members of the team die. Indigenous people find the remains of those left behind and bury them near the river, which they call River of the Strangers.

1686: John Abraham discovers the Churchill River and names it after Lord Churchill, the governor of the Hudson's Bay Company at that time.

1689: Henry Kelsey builds the first Fort Churchill; the fort burns down a year later.

1731: Fort Prince of Wales is planned; also planned is the fort at Cape Merry, now a popular tourist site.

1770-71: Samuel Hearne sets out on his famous trip to the Coppermine River in the Northwest Territories, across the Barren Lands, returning 18 months later.

1771: Fort Prince of Wales is finished.

1911: The contract to build rail tracks between The Pas and Churchill is signed; construction is completed in 1929.

1912: The borders defining the province of Manitoba are established.

1942-44: About 200 members of the U.S. Army take up duty in Churchill; construction of the new fort and the airport.

1957: The Rocket Range Center is built as a center for research into the northern lights as part of the geophysical year.

1976: Founding of the Churchill Northern Studies Center for ongoing scientific research by university students.

1980-81: The whole of Fort Churchill, including all living quarters and barracks, is leveled. Today, the foundations are still visible.

An aerial view of Fort Prince of Wales, completed in 1771. Arctic explorer Samuel Hearne passed through the region a year earlier on a tour of the Barren Lands and the tundra en route to the Arctic Ocean. Today, the fort is a favorite destination for Manitoba tourists.

The Polar Bears of Hudson Bay

Playful Fights

Mock fights are one of the most impressive pastimes shared among the young male polar bears at Churchill. Standing erect on hind legs, these white giants often engage in hours of good-natured wrestling, taking turns biting an opponent's ears and neck, then dragging him to the ground. The bears tumble about on the snow like a pair of well-choreographed Hollywood stunt men, sending fresh powder off their thick coats and into the air in long streams of glistening crystals. Just as quickly, they'll bounce to their feet and start a shoving match or a fistfight.

It is not unusual to see one panting bear, weary from a confrontation, licking snow to quench his thirst, while his opponent lies spread-eagled on the ice to cool his tummy. Quickly recovering, however, each launches a fresh attack, and the bout begins anew. Fair weather has little to do with the scheduling of these ritual matches: one evening in the blinding haze from fiercely drifting snow, I barely made out the silhouettes of two bears play-fighting.

For juveniles, such encounters help to hone the skills necessary to survive the battles they will face later in life for mates, territory and food. For adults that already know their way around, however, the meaning of these extended play sessions between individuals which will become deadly rivals during breeding season remains a matter of speculation. Some scientists suggest that play may be purely circumstantial—a kind of when-in-Rome philosophy—while others argue that play may give even the most experienced bears an opportunity to assess the competition long before any real fight, where the stakes are high.

Before sunrise one morning, I returned to the spot where I had last seen my polar pugilists of the day before. The sky, which had cleared overnight, was turning bright red as I noticed the duo lying peacefully on the ice. Spent from a recent bout, they were eating generous helpings of snow to cool down, even as the fiery red sun peeked over the horizon. Moments later, the bears rose to their feet and began flailing outstretched forelegs, aiming to land a decisive blow. But after a few lackluster jabs, each retreated to a favorite snowdrift and flopped down for a well-earned rest.

Mighty jaws, snowshoe-sized paws and a relentless, scrappy attitude all come into play during the polar bears' endless tundra tussles.

Adapting to the Arctic

Shaped by thousands of years of natural history, the polar bear is an arctic specialist, uniquely adapted to survive in the perpetually challenging environment of the North. Good insulation provides the first line of defense against the cold, and *Ursus maritimus* wears a warm "coat" comprising three layers: dense fur (guard hairs and a thick underwool that traps heat), skin and fat. The hollow surface guard hairs work like a solar collector, directing the sun's warm rays onto the bear's light-absorbing black skin. When densely packed together, these hairs form a coat in a range of vanilla, creamy and pale yellow hues. Adding up to four inches of cold-fighting protection, this coat amply protects the polar bear from fierce blizzards and the icy polar waters in which it swims.

Evidence of the polar bear's efficient insulation came to light unexpectedly a few years ago, when a scientist was attempting to take aerial photographs of suspected bear habitats using infrared film. Infrared film is highly sensitive to thermal radiation and is therefore an almost foolproof way to document the movements of warm-blooded animals. Yet the only sign of bears the photographs showed was the thermal imaging of their breath. While the results were disappointing for the polar bear census takers, this exercise inadvertently demonstrated that the hardy carnivore is remarkably well insulated and radiates almost none of its precious body heat.

From the soles of its feet to the tips of its ears, the polar bear has evolved to cope with the cold. A polar bear's foot pads not only are rough enough to provide traction but are thickly furred and immune to frostbite, while its ears are threaded with a fine network of blood vessels that transport sufficient thermal energy to the exposed auricles.

Acute senses and agility further distinguish the polar bear's survival skills on the arctic terrain. Its sense of smell is phenomenal: It can detect young seals hiding in a snow cave buried under three feet of snow nearly a mile away. Its vision, which tends to be farsighted, allows the bear to scan the endless landscape, while its hearing is comparable to that of humans.

In addition, polar bears are masters at negotiating thin ice. One October day, I watched a 3-year-old juvenile bear standing in a puddle of water in the middle of an ice-covered lake. Two days earlier, the frozen surface had been thick enough to support the bear's substantial weight, but the weather had since changed, as evidenced by the deep-

Ringed and bearded seals are the polar bear's dietary mainstay during the frigid arctic winter. Thousands of seals inhabit the cold, clear northern waters.

throated crackle that rang out with each of the bear's tentative steps. The ice was growing thinner by the hour.

The bear carefully spread its front legs out from either side of its body and pushed off gently with its hind legs, cautiously shuffling forward across the frozen lake like a novice ice skater. Sensing an imminent collapse, however, the bear momentarily stopped in its tracks and desperately tried spreading its hind legs to distribute its weight further. But it was for naught. The young bear's right front paw had already started to sink. In an instant, the bear carefully dropped into a full spread eagle and tried to slide forward, using its front paws like outriggers for stability and its claws for much-needed traction. When the ambitious young Nanook was within a few yards of solid ground, the whole surface gave way, and the bear took an unexpected dip in the frigid water. Unfazed by the outcome, it waded to shore and shook the water from its coat, not unlike the family dog after a swim in the lake.

Why Do the Polar Bears Come to Churchill?

Nowhere is nature's endless cycle more graphically illustrated than in the life of Nanook. While its southern cousins are snoozing the late winter away, the polar bear is at the peak of its activity—with the exception of pregnant females, which must set up dens to wait out the cold. Thanks to its carnivorous disposition, the polar bear spends the winter roaming about on the vast ice pack in search of a steady supply of high-protein meals.

Two of the most vital feeding sites for foraging bears are areas of open water, known as polynyas, and leads, which are ice-free stretches of water that follow a coastline in linear fashion and teem with arctic wildlife. The entire perimeter of Hudson Bay, for example, is outlined by a lead created by strong winds, currents and tidal motions, while a similar and much larger system completely encircles the polar basin in the high Arctic. (Russian explorer and biologist Savva Uspenskii named the latter system the Arctic Ring of Life, because of its unparalleled significance in the cycle of polar ecosystems.) Polynyas, on the other hand, are irregularly shaped arctic ponds that range in size from a few hundred square yards to hundreds of square miles.

The same tidal forces that keep polynyas and leads free of ice also stir up the rich organic nutrients from the water column which support

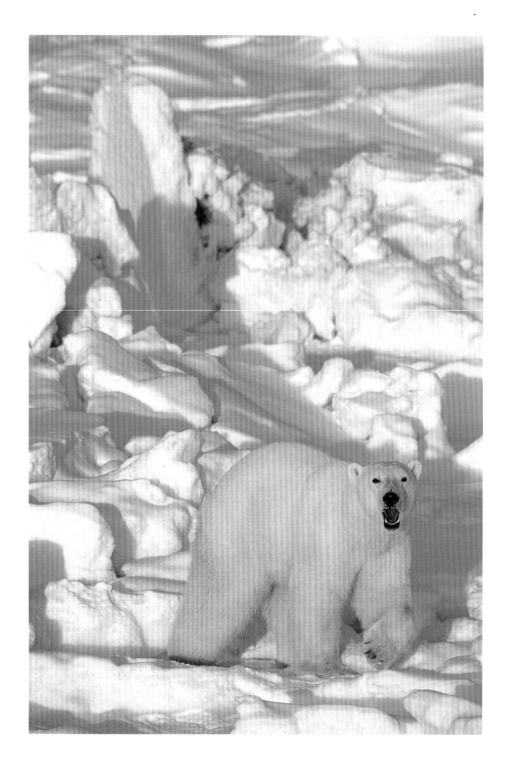

plankton, the building block in the pelagic food chain. As a result, these areas are critical for the survival of many arctic species. Birds rely on them early in their breeding season, when no other sources of food are available. Marine mammals such as seals and walruses, which need access to both water and air, can always be spotted nearby. It is little wonder that these hotbeds of wildlife activity—located in roughly the same area year after year—are popular among hungry polar bears.

By June and July, however, the pack ice in Hudson Bay begins to break up, and free-floating sheets with polar bears on board drift on southerly winds to James Bay. Once wedged into this southern appendix of the great inland sea, the massive icy rafts dissolve, leaving the stranded bears to swim to shore in the direction of Churchill. Facing a long wait until the next winter, polar bears, in contrast to brown and black bears, begin to live largely off their fat reserves. They sleep or lounge during the day to conserve energy, often resting in beds dug into the cool earth to escape from the legions of parasitic insects that swarm throughout the North during summer.

In these lazy summer days, polar bears are equally relaxed in their culinary preferences, exploiting a diverse range of prey from mice, gophers, lemmings, bird eggs and nestlings to seal and beluga carcasses that wash ashore. In August and September, sweet summer berries are a readily available main-course item for the hungry bears as they start their trek northward. Following the coast in search of the site of an early freeze, they reach Churchill by mid-October, where they wait for the ice to form a pathway to their delectable seal meals.

The geographic layout of the coast in the Churchill area acts as a magnet for polar bears; the region's tides, winds, currents and temperatures combine to speed up the ice-forming process. Running almost straight north and south, the Hudson Bay coastline takes a sharp turn east at Churchill, where a landmass protrudes into Hudson Bay and forms an upturned hook. In October, strong winds push new ice that

Over the course of the winter, foraging polar bears wander hundreds of miles across the Hudson Bay ice. Individuals have been found on the Quebec coast of this great inland sea, 500 miles east of Churchill.

is forming up north along the coast in a southerly direction, where it quickly accumulates, along with locally forming young ice, in the shallow water of the Churchill hook.

The cycle isn't complete, however, until the open waters of Hudson Bay freeze over, a process that can take from two days (as was the case in 1991) to two weeks. By late October or early November, strong winds from the north drive air temperatures down to minus 5 degrees F. This flash-freezing is accompanied by high winds (35-50 mph) that blow heavy snow across the water and send icy 12-foot waves crashing onto the rocky shore. As crystals form, the bay's surface is transformed into a heavy slush. Once the temperature drops below minus 4 degrees F, the retreating tide deposits the first solid crust of ice along the coast. At the same time, the motion of the incoming tide, like a hydraulic compactor, forces any young ice inland, where it forms a solid foundation that becomes the most sought-after new habitat for the hungry bears. On some days, up to 200 polar bears can be seen from the air in the coastal regions between Cape Churchill and the town proper.

Within a few nights of this dramatic metamorphosis, Hudson Bay has assumed its winter mantle—an uninterrupted white vista to the limits of the horizon. Through my binoculars, however, I can just make out several cream-colored dots in the distance: The polar bears are leaving the land once more to close the annual circle of arctic life.

A nearby disturbance or the threat of danger for her young cubs sends a female polar bear up on her hind legs to get a better view. At its full height, a polar bear may stand 10 feet tall, an intimidating sight for an approaching intruder.

Venturing too far out onto new ice, this young bear, despite its excellent sense of balance, repeatedly broke through the surface. When it eventually reached stronger ice, the bear was able to pull itself out of the water. Polar bears are superb swimmers and divers, and this one seemed to enjoy the periodic ice-cold dips.

During the transitional season, before the polar bears return to the sea ice, food shortages can reduce even the most powerful bears to hunting for mice.

A polar bear takes a refreshing roll on the snowy ground.

A Show of Strength
Two white giants challenge each other
during a blustery snowstorm.

28

Polar Bear

Zoological Classification
Class: Mammalia
Order: Carnivora
Family: Ursidae
Genus: *Ursus*
Species: *maritimus*

Body Measurements
Length: males, 94 to 98 inches;
females, 71 to 83 inches
Shoulder height: up to 63 inches
Standing erect: up to 130 inches
Length of tail: $2^3/_4$ to $4^3/_4$ inches

Typical Features
Stretched body; low shoulders; strongly
developed hindquarters; long and rather slim
neck; web-footed plantigrade, web along half
length of toes; glossy yellow-white coat;
hibernating animal.

Way of Living and Habitat
Solitary animal; young live with mother;
inhabits arctic region and south rim of
arctic pack ice.

Food
Mainly seals, stranded whales and walruses,
carcasses, human refuse and, during the
summer, plants, grasses and berries.

Reproduction
Mating season: from the end of May until
early June.
Gestation: about 8 months; 1 to 4 cubs
(normally 2); at birth, the cubs are the size
of a large rat (1-2 lb); they are born blind
and deaf.

Course of Life
Cubs separate from their mother at about
2.5 years; pubescence between 3 and 5 years;
maximum age is unknown.

Enemies
For adult bears, none aside from humans;
young bears are occasionally attacked and
killed by older male bears.

Population
The worldwide polar bear population is
thought to be between 7,000 and 20,000
—some estimates range as high as 40,000—
following a strong decline to about 5,000
bears after the war. Polar bears enjoy total
protection in the Russian arctic region.
Controlled hunting is exercised on the North
American continent and in Scandinavia.

Previous pages: Overheated after a demanding first round of play-fighting, the bears lower their temperatures by either lying flat, rolling about on the cool ground or taking a refreshing plunge into the icy water.

Right: The largest predator on Earth, a male polar bear can weigh well over 1,000 pounds and live for 25 years.

Right: From time to time, the vigilant bear raises its nose to the wind, relying on its keen sense of smell to pick up the scent of prey or an approaching intruder.

Sun Worshiper
A sunbathing bear holds its head high as flakes of drifting snow settle lightly on its face.

Polar bears have little trouble finding a place to sleep. Three thick insulating layers—fur, skin and fat—help prevent the loss of precious body heat when the bear curls up on the open ground. Even when completely covered with snow, the bear releases so little heat that the snow on its back does not melt.

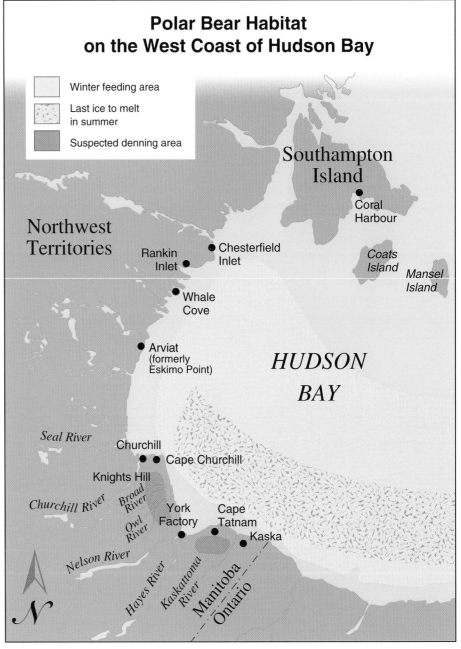

Polar Bear Habitat on the West Coast of Hudson Bay

Winter feeding area

Last ice to melt in summer

Suspected denning area

Southampton Island

Coral Harbour

Northwest Territories

Rankin Inlet

Chesterfield Inlet

Coats Island

Mansel Island

Whale Cove

Arviat (formerly Eskimo Point)

HUDSON BAY

Seal River

Churchill

Cape Churchill

Knights Hill

Churchill River

Broad River

Owl River

York Factory

Cape Tatnam

Kaska

Nelson River

Hayes River

Kaskattoma River

Manitoba

Ontario

N

Mice and lemmings are not safe from a hungry bear, even when scurrying between rocks.

Right: Stretching and bending after a long snooze, this bear is ready for another day.

A challenge to another wrestling match.

An alert mother uses her body to shield her 9-month-old cub from an approaching full-grown male.

Spring and Summertime

Safe and Secure With the Family: Polar Bears and Their Young

During April and May, polar bears mate. Female polar bears are known as induced ovulators, which means that they don't routinely ovulate but rely instead on the mating ritual to stimulate ovulation. To ensure that mating is successful, partners stay together for an entire week.

Polar bear courtship and mating take place on the sea ice and are synchronous with the birth of thousands of seal pups that are ideal fare for the expectant *Ursus maritimus*. At birth, the awkwardly immobile seals weigh from about 9 to 11 pounds, but within a few weeks, they balloon to 55 to 65 pounds, with 75 percent of their nutritional content available to the polar bear as high-calorie fat. Lacking in neither culinary ambition nor hunting prowess, a polar bear also typically feeds on prey such as a 450-pound walrus, which it can kill with a single blow of its massive paw.

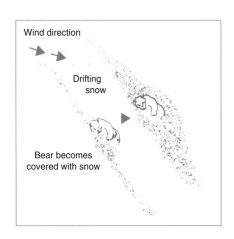

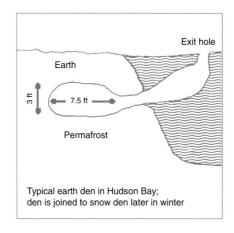

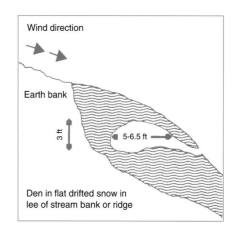

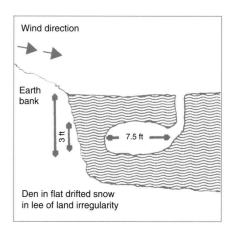

By mid- to late June, when the bears leave the ice for the season, females have often tripled or quadrupled their weight. A few years ago, researchers documented one such remarkable example of weight gain. Caught in the late fall, a young female weighed in at a svelte 210 pounds. When the same bear was caught and weighed at the end of the spring, she tipped the scales at 990 pounds. This substantial weight increase is essential for the survival of the pregnant females, which will den during the winter and nurse their young for at least five months before being able to hunt again.

Right: In the Hudson Bay area, polar bear cubs stay with their mother for up to two years, nursing during the entire time. After that, the young bears set out on their own.

The Bears' Den

In anticipation of the arrival of her offspring, which takes place anytime within a 195-to-260-day interval, the expectant polar bear spends some time searching for a suitable cave or snowdrift in which she can excavate a comfortable 6-by-10-by-4-foot den. An aggregation of such birthing dens is known as a denning area. Scientists believe that either inherited traditions or proximity to a polynya may be the key factors in the denning popularity of certain regions. While scientists have accounted for 17 different denning areas across the entire Arctic, the one near Churchill, Manitoba, discovered in 1969, is considered the largest in Canada. Located some 40 miles south of town—between Cape Churchill and the mouth of the Nelson River (see map on page 38)—the denning area is the birthing ground of choice for some 150 female bears.

Drifting in and out of sleep in her secure *igloovikus*, as Inuit call it, the female polar bear gives birth to her young sometime between November and February. Twins and triplets make up the typical polar bear family; only one litter of four has ever been documented. At birth, the polar bear cub is smaller than a small tree squirrel, weighing less than two pounds. Covered only with a light down, the newborn cub—its eyes still sealed shut—is completely helpless. In this undeveloped condition, the cubs are vulnerable to the cold. For their first three weeks of life, the mother remains inside the den with her youngsters, which curl up on her thighs for protection from the frigid ground.

Helpless though they may be during these early weeks, newborn cubs are equipped with long, pointed claws that enable them to comb through their mother's thick fur to reach her nipples. Polar bears produce the fattiest milk among bears—about 40 percent fat—which aids in the cubs' rapid development. The texture of the milk, like that of condensed milk, is thick and viscous, and its taste apparently ranges from bland to fishy, possibly influenced by the mother's diet.

After one month on their high-fat liquid menu, the cubs begin to crawl. At 6 weeks of age, they are able to open their eyes fully, and at 10 weeks, when they can keep their balance, they are ready to venture outside the den. Around this same time, the days start to get longer and warmer, and the mother herself crawls outside to stretch her limbs and shake off her winter slumber. After a few solo outings, she entices her chubby (by now weighing 25 pounds) and reluctant cubs to follow her out into the world, where they will enter their first—and most critical—season of life. Initially, the cubs restrict their play to the vicinity of the den, in case danger or bad weather demands a hasty retreat. But acclimatization to the winter environment is part of arctic life, and the quicker the cubs adapt, the better their long-term chances for survival.

Mother and babies start their long walk to the ice after a few days of frolicking close to home. Inuit call this journey *ah-tik-tok* ("those who wander to the sea"), and with the Churchill denning area some 40 to 60 miles from the coast, the trek is a hardship for a nursing mother that has been fasting for eight months. Nevertheless, she sets out at a steady pace, ever watchful for stragglers and always allowing adequate time for her offspring to nurse and rest.

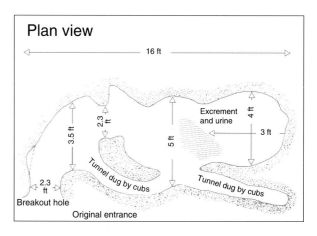

Plan view

Polar bears possess a remarkable sense of smell. Across a great distance, they can pick up the scent of seals in their snow covers. With their noses outstretched, these three are unable to follow the trail of the scent because the ice is not yet thick enough to support their weight.

Early to rise, two large polar bears start the day with a predawn tussle.

A November Morning
Right: A polar bear mother and her cubs wander across the endless Hudson Bay icefields.

After three or four days of traversing frozen lakes and negotiating ditches filled with fresh powdered snow, the family reaches the shore. The mother immediately starts to hunt for her first winter feast of seal. At this time of year, the mother and her young will eat only the high-calorie skin and fat and leave the rest of the carcass for scavengers, such as ravens, arctic foxes and glaucous gulls. The family remains together for 1½ to 2 years (up to 2½ years in the more northerly regions), with the cubs nursing throughout this period. When they do leave their mothers, juvenile polar bears often travel together, like roving bands of teenagers, until they are mature enough to start their own families at the age of 5.

Like all rambunctious youngsters, Nanook cubs are always in the mood for play. Despite their youthful antics, however, they are completely dependent on their mother for protection, warmth and food.

*Right: Regular companions of **Ursus maritimus**, arctic foxes follow close behind to feed on the remains of polar bear kills. Occasionally, however, a fox moves in too close and must then make a dash for its life.*

The Joys of Motherhood
Unable to leave her offspring to hunt for food, a mother bear continues to nurse her 9-month-old cub during the long wait until the ice affords her access to the delectable seals of the bay. Although the young bears gradually begin to eat solid food, they continue to nurse until the age of 18 to 24 months. I've made many trips to Hudson Bay, but this is the only time I was able to photograph the intimacy between a mother and her cub.

Siesta in the Snow
Right: Exhausted from nursing, a baby curls up with its mother for an afternoon nap amid the sparse tundra grasses.

Momentarily airborne with a surge of adrenaline, a protective mother bear charges toward a female adult that has wandered too near. A few warning nips display her strength and free both families to continue on their way. Polar bears have split-second reactions and are extremely fast runners for their size. Over a short distance, they can reach speeds of 30 miles per hour.

A Visit to the Polar Bear Babies

I waited a long time to ascend the list of the privileged few who are invited to travel with Canadian Wildlife Service (CWS) researchers and see a family of polar bears in action. In February 1993, my dream came true. I finally received a message from the CWS, which oversees the scientific investigation of *Ursus maritimus*: Weather permitting, I was next in line to join a trip by helicopter to the Churchill denning area. It was a long shot, I suppose, given that I was in Germany at the time, but it was also the chance I had been waiting for. I immediately booked a reservation aboard a plane bound for Churchill.

The weather conditions for a safe helicopter flight have to be nearly perfect—clear, windless, sunny, with a temperature no colder than minus 13 degrees F. So when southern Hudson Bay greeted me with its predictably unpredictable weather, and we were placed on standby, I began to experience a familiar sinking feeling.

Starting on February 26, I began my morning ritual of calls: first to the weather station, then to the scientists at the CWS. Every day, I sheepishly asked: "Today?"

And each day, the response to my hesitant inquiry was the same: "Sorry, not today."

Too afraid to leave my hotel in case the weather cleared up and I missed "the call," I had no opportunity to wander far from my post, whether to photograph the northern lights or simply to enjoy a trip on a dogsled.

I was on the verge of giving up, when a sunny springlike March 18 brought the good news: "We can take off!" Before I knew it, pilot Steve "The Eagle" Miller had taken me and Dennis Andriashek—a longtime collaborator of Dr. Ian Stirling at the CWS—up into the wild blue yonder.

The countryside whizzed past beneath us in a green-and-white patchwork stitched together from the alternating fabrics of conifers and snow. We crossed the tree line to the south and followed the route of a meandering creek, where we noticed large snowdrifts deposited on the lee side, an ideal location for polar bear dens. When Steve suddenly spied bear tracks directly below, he executed a steep descending turn that

Researchers use a simple hand scale to weigh the chubby polar bear cubs.

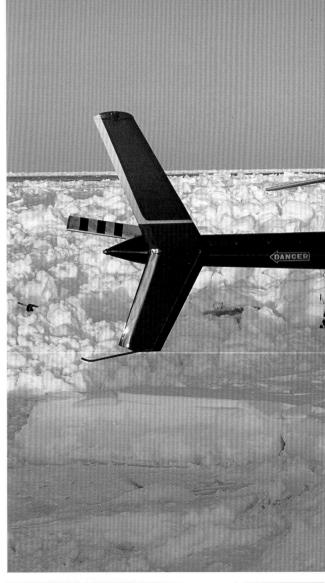

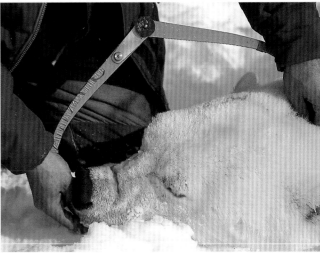

Over the past 10 years, helicopter pilot Steve "The Eagle" Miller has carried Canadian Wildlife Service scientists from Manitoba and the Northwest Territories to study more than 2,600 polar bears, making him the preeminent Canadian helicopter pilot in the harsh arctic environment.

It was a lucky turn of events for researchers when Miller, a onetime agriculture student, earned his flying license, sold his farm and took to the skies. He flew his first flight in 1982 with mammalogist Malcolm Ramsay of the University of Saskatchewan to find, identify and tag polar bears. Skill and precision in this treacherous occupation make Miller an indispensable partner to scientists traveling in the Arctic.

Above: A free-floating sheet of ice becomes our landing pad amid the endless pack ice.

Left: Gauging calipers are used to measure the size of the head of a tranquilized mother bear.

Right: A close inspection of this polar bear's paw reveals the stout meat-hook-like claws that enable her to drag a 100-pound seal through its breathing hole in the ice or to dig the family's sleeping cave through densely packed snow and frozen ground.

provided me with a momentary flashback to my morning meal.

Flying close to the tops of the highest trees near the creek, we were able to monitor the tracks of the bears. "There she is," I heard Dennis say through the earphones. "She's sticking her head out of the den. And look! There's a young one." As we banked to the right and resumed our search (the ground crew already having located this family), I was struck at once by how highly elusive these maternal groups are, even in the most heavily populated denning habitat in the country.

We continued our flight in hourly intervals, frequently stopping to refuel at designated depots along the way. After more than three hours in the air, we began to search along the ice ridge near the shore. Immediately, we saw tracks. Another eaglelike aerobatic maneuver downward, and Dennis called out: "In front! A large female with one, two…no…*three* cubs!"

As we circled over the pack ice for a few minutes, planning our landing, I enjoyed some of the most impressive views that I have ever seen. The sun, low on the horizon, filtered a reddish glow across the abstract sculptures of ice as the mother led her three cubs, single file, through the field of towering colored blocks toward the open water. In one unforgettable image of family bonding, two of the little bears left the track and clambered onto an iceberg; when the mother noticed their antics, she quickly ambled toward them and reared up on her hind legs, nuzzling her rambunctious babies nose to nose as though affectionately congratulating them on their caper.

*Ears stained with blood from a recent run-in with its siblings, a 3-month-old cub takes a refreshing milk break. Fat is an essential element of the polar bear's diet from birth onward, and the milk of a lactating **Ursus maritimus** is the richest among bears. According to researchers, polar bear milk varies in taste from bland to fishy.*

I was jolted out of my wildlife reverie by my companions, who reminded me that it was time to get down to work. Before we could make an approach, however, the mother bear would have to be stunned with a tranquilizer. But she was on the run, and Steve had to position the helicopter directly above her, close enough so that Dennis could accurately direct the dart at her muscular shoulder. After he fired, we immediately veered away, observing the family from a safe distance. The big female con-

tinued to lumber far out onto the pack ice, but the tranquilizer soon took effect, and her gallop gradually slowed to a weary saunter until, finally, she stopped in her tracks and slumped into a deep sleep.

Steve landed the helicopter on a sheet of ice with the skids parked with only a few inches of room on either side. As we left the chopper and skated along the slippery ice to the bear family, some 60 feet away, it was hard to tell whether we were free-floating or firmly attached to the other nearby pack ice. At that moment, I suddenly experienced a heightened awareness of my own precarious position: two cameras strung around my neck, one hand holding the tripod and the other clutching my photographer's bag. What would happen if I slipped?

Happily, I didn't. But by then, it was late in the afternoon, and with the temperature falling each minute, the work itself was no cakewalk. I quickly shot a few frames of the bears and their surroundings as Dennis and Steve began their work.

The first task at hand was to leash the frightened cubs to prevent them from making a futile dash across the ice that would spell their certain deaths. Next, Steve inspected the mother's body and found her coat was soiled from the long months in the den, her fur littered with balls of frosted ice that he carefully cut free. After measuring the length of the bear's body and the breadth of her chest (these figures could then be calculated into a rough weight), he confirmed her identity by comparing the number on a plastic ear tag to the number tattooed inside her lip. Entered into a thick registry for quick reference, like a telephone book, these numbers are part of an international system of identifying individual bears.

As Dennis extracted a small tooth, he explained that laboratory technicians would be able to determine the bear's exact age by cutting the tooth into thin disks, thereby exposing its annual growth rings. Dennis and Steve then took blood and milk samples and gave the bear a final once-over for signs of illness or injury. Before we departed, however, the researchers sedated the cubs, ensuring that the family would stay together until each member was alert, and unleashed them. In a few hours, the mother and her babies would awaken and continue on their journey across the ice.

A Life at Risk

Even in their remote habitat, polar bears face a number of dangers. All polar bears are vulnerable to the effects of environmental pollution, such as petroleum spills and global warming, which can result in irreversible damage to their habitat and ultimately their lives. Human hunters and poachers are a menace to adult bears, but more important, if the kill also leaves orphaned and helpless cubs, hunting threatens populations.

In their day-to-day lives, however, polar bear cubs are at greatest risk from adult males, which stand to increase their own reproductive success by eliminating unrelated cubs. Once a family of polar bears reaches the ice and the vicinity of the feeding grounds, the mother must protect her young, and she often positions them in a secluded area. Incidents of attacks on cubs by aggressive males have been reported by Inuit over the years. Some one hundred years ago, Nobel Prize winner and Arctic explorer Fridtjof Nansen of Norway witnessed a large male bear kill two cubs that were feeding on a seal. Likewise, packs of wolves occasionally attempt to separate cubs from their mother to kill them. While no eyewitness accounts exist to date, a cub carcass encircled by wolf tracks was recorded by two hunters in 1993 near Cape Churchill.

Left: All white fur with dramatic black features, cuddly-looking twins curl up side by side on their sleeping mother's back.

Overleaf, left: With chunks of ice still frozen to her back, a mother bear leads her twins onto the pack ice. Wanderers on the ice are called **ah-tik-tok** *among Inuit, a phrase that typically describes polar bear families during the late-fall and winter months.*

Overleaf, right: Shards of sheet ice make ideal platforms for seal-hunting polar bears during March.

This 3-month-old polar bear cub has just emerged from its family den.

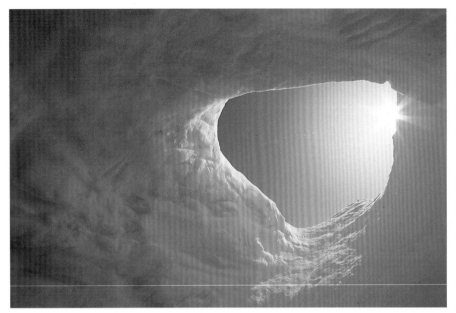

Left: A polar bear cub spends the first few months of its life in a "nursery" hollowed out of snow. In late November, in anticipation of the birth of her young, the pregnant female digs the modest cave in a hard-packed snowdrift. Some etchings from the mother's claws are visible on the walls of the snow cave.

Right: Playing with a broken branch, a polar bear cub demonstrates its curious and mischievous nature.

Triplets are the exception to the rule in polar bear families. In most cases, only two cubs will survive to this stage.

The Return of the Snow Geese

In the south, there are tangible signs of spring during the month of May. The trees are covered with young leaves and fragrant blossoms, while chattering birds are busy building their nests. But well into the middle of the same month on ice-covered Hudson Bay, the temperature barely nudges above freezing, and on a typical day, bristling cold winds still send threatening snow clouds sailing across the sky.

On rare occasions, however, one can enjoy a glimpse of brighter days to come. The cloud cover parts briefly, and the sun, a radiant crystal adorning the blue sky, sends warming rays to Earth. When the winds finally shift and the all-too-familiar northerly gusts change to lilting southerly breezes, they carry with them the faint sounds of distant honking. It is the seasonal migration of the snow geese (*Chen caerulescens*), and their annual air show heralds the arrival of spring in the North.

Following their aerial highway, snow geese migrate across the endless coastal ice ranges to their breeding grounds in the North.

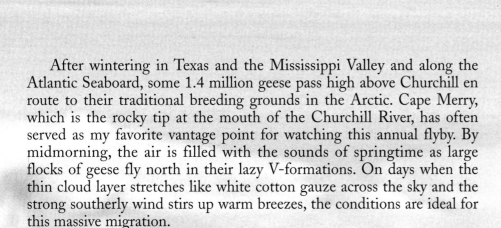

After wintering in Texas and the Mississippi Valley and along the Atlantic Seaboard, some 1.4 million geese pass high above Churchill en route to their traditional breeding grounds in the Arctic. Cape Merry, which is the rocky tip at the mouth of the Churchill River, has often served as my favorite vantage point for watching this annual flyby. By midmorning, the air is filled with the sounds of springtime as large flocks of geese fly north in their lazy V-formations. On days when the thin cloud layer stretches like white cotton gauze across the sky and the strong southerly wind stirs up warm breezes, the conditions are ideal for this massive migration.

Exploiting the strong air currents and buoyant thermals, the large assemblies of white- and blue-phase birds fly high in the air on five-foot-wide wings toward their northern destination. As many as 150 geese make up each individual flock, and sometimes, I get the im-

pression that they take their lead from flocks of Canada geese (*Branta canadensis*), Ross' geese (*Chen rossii*) or sandhill cranes (*Grus canadensis*) that likewise fill the air. Traveling noisily along the aerial pathway, the cranes drown out the shrill falsetto of the snow geese with their brassy trumpeting.

La Pérouse Bay, east of Churchill, is one of the best-known breeding grounds for snow geese. As soon as they arrive, the birds establish their nests in colonies. The female lines a shallow depression in the flat tundra with a sprinkling of dry grasses and her own down. She then incubates a clutch of four or five eggs for a brief 21 to 25 days, as the male remains dutifully close at hand. In another 40 days, the little goslings are able to fly.

If there is an unexpected drop in temperature and the winds begin to blow from the north, thousands of geese will interrupt their flight and

return to the wet area and shoreline near Churchill. When this occurs, the regions of Goose Creek Road and Bird Cove take on a distinct speckled texture when viewed from the air. On one such day, I decided to take aerial photographs of flying geese and of those resting on the nearby mud flats.

Bush pilot Bruce Martin maneuvered his little Cessna along the runway to the starting position and revved the engine. Taxiing only a short distance, the compact plane quickly leapt into the air, and within minutes, we were soaring over the first flock of birds. Far below, I could see a thick ice pack still covering the river and only the rare dark spot where a stream of melting water twisted through the icy barrier. Amid the kaleidoscope of color, the dark water reflected images from the sky overhead.

When I opened the window to get a better view with my camera, the cozy quiet of the cockpit was shattered by a gale-force blast. Looking through the viewfinder, I saw an impressionistic countryside 500 feet below and large flocks of snow geese and Canada geese suspended over the river on their route north. We followed, hot on their trail, across Button Bay to the North Knife River delta, a few miles away. Beginning its course in the deep woods and lakes of northern Manitoba, near the Saskatchewan border, the river ends in an array of meandering channels, swampy areas and tundra that is an El Dorado of sweet grasses and plants for water birds making their way north. From my bird's-eye view, I could see countless waterfowl—Canada geese interspersed with ducks and snow geese—that would share the bounty of this unscheduled stopover. After a short one-hour flight, we returned to Churchill.

The Ice Breaks

Early June marks the beginning of one of the most beautiful seasons on the west coast of Hudson Bay. Change is in the air, and every part of the region from the landscape to the flora and fauna undergoes a profound transformation. Each day is renewed by 18 hours of sorely missed sunlight, and even the night, which is no longer shrouded in complete darkness, glows with the hint of twilight. It is also the time when raptors, waterfowl and shorebirds arrive in Churchill by the millions: ruddy turnstones, Bonaparte's, Sabine's and Ross' gulls, terns, loons, eiders, pintails, teals, mallards and mergansers.

Between Cape Merry and Fort Prince of Wales, the Churchill River swells to nearly one mile across and is choked with icebergs. In some

Previous page: Casting long, dark shadows onto the fractured icefields below, loose formations of snow geese fly across the frozen Churchill River in May. Upon their arrival in the Arctic, the birds immediately begin their courtship and breeding cycle.

areas, the winter's 10-foot-thick ice layer breaks up in a rapid week-long icy exodus that sends remnant calves of the winter season floating to Hudson Bay. At low tide, the sunlight reflects a brilliantly colored orange off the ice walls that hang tenaciously over the open river, while freshly melted water wears away hidden channels inside the ice, releasing a golden curtain of water into the riverbed. Downstream, larger icebergs inside Hudson Bay take several weeks longer to melt, and by mid-July, giant blocks still dot the bay, reminders of the ever-changing weather picture.

As I know now, the region's unpredictable weather can wreak havoc with the plans of an arctic visitor. I have also learned that these climatic contrasts can play tricks with the mind as well. During a trip along the rocky coast in late May, I experienced a spectacular optical phenomenon, observing what appeared to be undulating masses of visible air, like giant atmospheric waves, colliding, toppling and crashing over the ice.

This unusual activity is, in fact, a consequence of temperature differentials. Above land, the air reaches 85 degrees F, while the air temperature over the ice is barely above freezing. My elevated vantage point offered an excellent view of the hot-air masses, which were defined by a clear border of shallow cold air over the ice. Wherever I turned my gaze, I saw the unbelievable.

Far out over the open areas of water between the ice packs, there appeared to be blocks of blue that became walls. Within a few seconds, the currents of air assumed the shapes of buildings, cars and trees stretched tall by the wafting air masses, flickering and ephemeral against the backdrop of the typically austere landscape. I was seeing a mirage! Light refracting through the column of hot and cold air was magnified and projected into these illusory shapes onto a horizon that continually shifted with my position. I dubbed the phenomenon "daytime northern lights."

A shimmering mirage that resembles an ancient stone city rises vertically from the ice on the distant horizon.

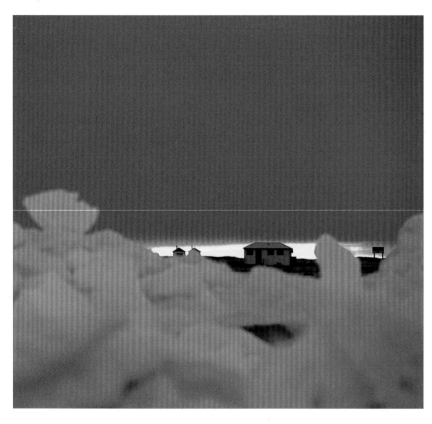

Icebergs drifting along the river are part of the ever-changing landscape near Churchill, Manitoba. They also herald the coming of spring and the arrival of tourists at nearby Fort Prince of Wales.

Thunderstorm in the Arctic

One afternoon in June 1993, I wandered through town, enjoying the gentle summer breeze and doing a little shopping. Within minutes, the warm gusts were transformed into a storm driven by 30-mile-per-hour winds. Like a hair dryer heating up with use, the air temperature climbed from 46 to 68 degrees F. Anticipating a summer tempest, I grabbed my photo gear and headed to the cape, where the wind's force was even more turbulent. Icebergs that had been locked against the rocky ground for weeks, dribbling weak streams of water, were in the throes of rapid dissolution, releasing cascades of spring runoff into the bay. I was surrounded by thunderous groans, as ice sheets fractured and caves collapsed around me.

Almost as quickly as it started, however, the storm subsided, but the air remained eerily warm until late in the evening. At 9 o'clock, thunderclouds gathered in the west and a towering gray wall approached the town. Instantly, a heavy curtain of fog fell over the river, enclosing most of the icebergs, which were illuminated by the first bolt of lightning etched across the sky. Without warning, I was caught in a pounding downpour. Though it washed away the fog and the heat, I was wet to the bone and sought shelter between the rocks as the thunderstorm passed overhead. For a few still minutes, the wind appeared to have died down. Then it struck again without warning, drenching me, my glasses and my camera lens with warm mist. I was unable to take another photograph.

A supercharged bolt of lightning touches down on the ice sheets of Hudson Bay. Thunderstorms are a rare event in the Arctic.

74

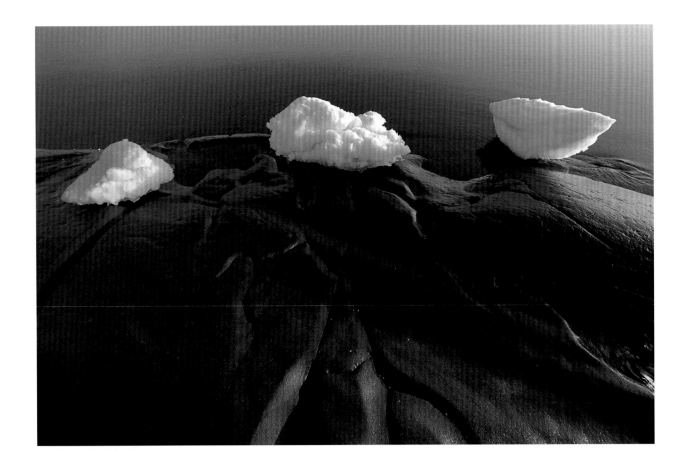

The rising sun on June 21, the longest day of the year, casts a spectral array of red, orange and blue light on the last tenacious ice sculptures of winter.

Previous pages: By the end of June, the Cape Merry sky during the small hours of the morning still glows with the red tones of twilight. The occasional splash of calving icebergs is the only interruption in the landscape's hypnotic quiet.

Meltwater dripping through the porous icebergs sculpts their walls into dramatic peaks and crevices.

A torrent of water released from a melting block of ice is illuminated by the reflected golden sunlight.

Courtship in the Cold
Norwegian polar explorer Fridtjof Nansen traveled in the Arctic
for years before he saw his first pair of Ross' gulls.

Pulsating Life: The Brief Arctic Summer

By mid-June, the land is alive with summer. Purple mountain saxifrage (*Saxifraga oppositifolia*) sheds its blossoms, while Lapland rosebay (*Rhododendron lapponicum*) blankets the tundra with an exotic red cover. With each passing day, the gradual appearance of colorful summer wildflowers, such as the white blossoms of the late-blooming northern lady's slipper (*Cypripedium passerinum*), brightens the harsh ground. The buzzing of insects fills the air.

The fauna, too, makes its presence felt. Avian families are abundant, with the Ross' gull (*Rhodostethia rosea*) standing out as the largest bird attraction during spring and summer. Seeing a Ross' gull is a rite of passage for travelers to the North. Even Norway's veteran polar explorer Fridtjof Nansen considered his first encounter with a Ross' gull as the fulfillment of a lifelong dream.

A rare springtime visitor to the most remote northern regions of Canada, the Ross' gull, which has typically bred in the grueling climate of northeastern Siberia, was first found near Churchill on June 10, 1980. This event was so rare that *Life* magazine featured the gull of the high Arctic on its cover. Since then, two pairs of Ross' gulls have continued to return to the marshy ponds just outside Churchill. Elusive as the birds may be, these stout-billed creatures, which resemble doves, show little fear of humans and allowed us to approach within arm's length.

Also breeding near the ponds at Churchill is the world-traveling arctic tern (*Sterna paradisaea*). A follower of the sun, this tern chases polar summers, logging some 22,000 miles on its annual round-trip migration from the Arctic to Antarctica and back again. One long-lived Arctic tern, estimated to be 27 years old, logged enough miles during its lifetime to equal the distance to the moon.

Just south of the tree line, the boreal forest offers the perfect breeding habitat for such majestic northern raptors as the great gray owl (*Strix nebulosa*) and the northern hawk owl (*Surnia ulula*). These devoted parents provide weeks of engaging entertainment for curious birders, which I learned firsthand in 1993 as I watched a pair of hawk owls working diligently to construct the elevated nests in which they incubate their eggs and feed their young.

Right: A male arctic tern offers his mate a freshly
caught fish as a courtship gift.

Competitors in the field, the graceful arctic terns arrive at Hudson Bay in June after making their herculean migration from Antarctica.

Courtship displays, such as the passing of food between mates, help strengthen the pair bond.

Ritualized behaviors are repeated numerous times to reinforce the pair's commitment to each other.

Belugas, the Canaries of the Sea

Belugas are among Hudson Bay's many summer guests. German naturalist Paul Pallas made the first sighting of these smooth, finless, creamy white whales during a trip to northern Russia, and hence their common name is derived from *belukha*, the Russian word for white. With the exception of one small southerly population of 500 whales that lives in the St. Lawrence River, *Delphinapterus leucas* occupies the circumpolar waters of Canada, the United States and Russia. Although the total population of belugas is unknown, estimates range between 40,000 and 55,000.

To keep warm in its frigid surroundings, the beluga relies on a thick layer of blubber, which accounts for some 40 percent of its body mass. It grows to 15 feet in length and weighs approximately 3,300 pounds. While the large baleen whales filter-feed on krill, copepods and schools of small fish, toothed whales such as the beluga selectively seize larger prey items—salmon and squid, octopus and other nonvertebrates. A flexible neck and head enable the beluga to turn from side to side and to look up and down; this not only helps the beluga snatch prey from the ocean floor but keeps it alert to approaching predators such as polar bears.

Delphinapterus leucas is a shallow-water specialist, and during the winter season, the beluga can be seen in the polynyas and leads of the ice-covered bay. (This preference for shallow water makes the beluga vulnerable to attack from polar bears.) In spring, however, belugas move to the warmer coastal waters of the Arctic and subarctic regions, a migratory behavior that is unique to northern-hemisphere individuals. While a few larger groups stay in Lancaster Sound and Prince Regent Inlet, near Baffin Island, other dense herds of the sociable belugas appear along the ice-free coast of Hudson Bay around mid-June. Thousands gather at the mouths of the Seal and Churchill rivers, where some use the rocky shallows and sand to shed their old skin, wildly threshing their tail fins and occasionally stretching their heads above the surface. In the quiet bays where fresh water and salt water mix, segregated groups of females that have been pregnant for 14 months give birth to their five-foot-long offspring. From the age of 5, females reproduce every two to three years during their 30-year life spans.

Only fully grown individuals exhibit the characteristic white skin of the beluga. Newborn calves are brown, and during the early part of their lives, their color continues to change through a variety of shades of gray. From the air, this range of colors helps me distinguish several large

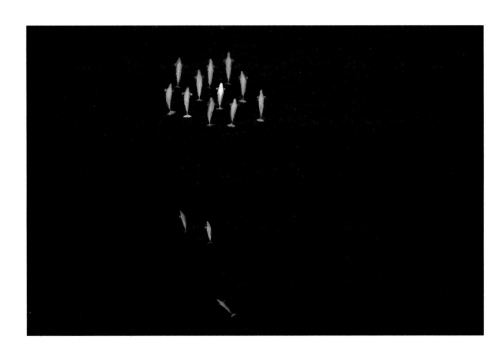

Early in June, family pods of white beluga whales gather at the mouths of the rivers that empty into Hudson Bay. There, in the chilly fresh water, they cast off their old skin, and the females give birth to five-foot-long calves.

white cows from their dark-skinned calves as they mill about in their pods. The sight of these highly social creatures reminds me that belugas, which converse in a lively manner with a variety of clicks, screams, whistles and trills, are thought to have the richest vocabulary of all whales. This chatter from the deep is sufficiently audible to humans that early whalers, who heard the sounds through the ship's hull, nicknamed the white whales "the canaries of the sea."

Right: Gordon Point, a long sand-and-gravel peninsula, reaches far out into Hudson Bay and provides an ideal breeding habitat for ground-nesting shorebirds.

Left: The first pair of breeding Ross' gulls known to nest in the Churchill area was observed in 1980. Since then, the birds have become a major attraction, drawing roughly 3,000 birders from around the world each year.

An arctic tern demonstrates its renowned assertiveness to a bird watcher who has come too close to the breeding grounds. Well-placed droppings on the interloper's hat and shoulders, the tern's first strategy of defense, were followed by a face-to-face confrontation that failed to intimidate the persistent human visitor. This photograph won First Prize for Humor at the international World Press Photo Competition in 1990.

Willow catkin.

Willow (Salix reticulata) in bloom.

Lichen-covered rocks.

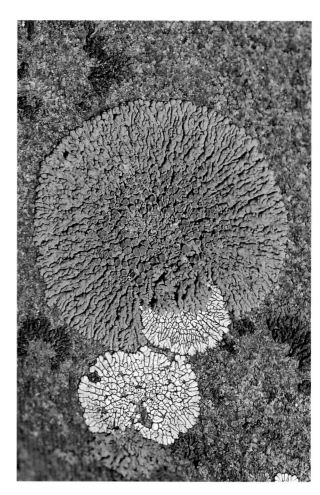

Right: During the summer, the sand-and-gravel beaches of Hudson Bay are transformed into colorful flower gardens. Dried stems, yellow blossoms and closed pods are all visible on this Arnica alpina.

A member of the extraordinary orchid family, the lady's slipper grows among the shrubby willows on the coast.

Photo: Joan Schweder

One of the fastest and most efficient ways to travel across the open tundra is in a four-wheeled all-terrain vehicle. Loaded with more than 1,000 pounds of equipment, this versatile vehicle can negotiate water, rocks, gravel and grassland.

The fuchsia-colored flower on the Lapland rosebay (**Rhododendron lapponicum**) adds an exotic hue to the lichen-covered ground.

Right: Large tracts of rocky Hudson Bay coastline are carpeted with colorful flora during the summer season, creating a vital habitat for a host of birds, insects and small mammals.

92

Right: The forested patchwork of islands along the North Knife River delta provides an ideal habitat for songbirds and mammals.

*The merlin (**Falco columbarius**), a bird of prey common to the northern region, specializes in small birds, mice and lemmings.*

Grimacing in reaction to the persistent cry of a hungry youngster, a northern hawk owl prepares to feed the fledgling. The young birds are mobile enough to leave the nests long before they are able to fly and spend their time perched on nearby branches, squawking to maintain parental contact and begging for food.

Right: The forward-facing eyes and hooked bill of this young northern hawk owl will contribute to its success as a hunter.

Overleaf, left: The young northern hawk owl's loud call is a dead giveaway to its hideout deep in the woods, where it perches on the decaying spire of an old tree.

Overleaf, right: Small birds and lemmings are devoured whole by the immature owls that are able to move beyond the nest.

The Arctic Fox: Northern Survival Expert

Like the polar bear, the arctic fox is a signature species of subarctic Hudson Bay. Because *Alopex lagopus* is such a superb example of an animal adapted to the arctic habitat, I looked forward to observing it in its natural surroundings—in both summer and winter. However, several solo trips to the tundra in the early summer of 1993 and numerous long-distance telephone calls from Churchill to more remote areas, where I had hoped to hear news of denning foxes, had proved fruitless. In July, I finally connected with Donald, a knowledgeable Inuit guide from Arviat (formerly Eskimo Point), who told me that he knew where to find a den occupied by a family of the northern canids.

Mating season for the arctic fox begins sometime in March or April, and about mid-May, the pregnant female starts to search out a suitable location in which to give birth to her litter of two-ounce pups. The month of July, therefore, would be a perfect time to visit the den, which should be busy with frolicking, photogenic young kits. Anticipating that the foxes would grow accustomed to nosy human neighbors, Donald decided to pitch a big tent in the vicinity of the den in advance of my arrival.

Arviat is located on the Hudson Bay coast, about 80 miles north of the border between Manitoba and the Northwest Territories. When I arrived, Donald and I loaded the necessary equipment and supplies onto a trailer, mounted a pair of fully packed Honda four-wheelers and headed overland to the west on the "Inuit Highway."

My earlier unsuccessful forays in search of arctic foxes had made me more anxious than usual, and I wondered aloud how Donald had located a den so quickly. He explained that foxes dig their dens in dry and slightly elevated ground. Near Arviat, apparently, these criteria are found in only one kind of landform—an esker. Much easier to dig through than wet, swampy tundra or rock-hard permafrost, eskers are soft ridges of loose sand and gravel left behind by receding glacial meltwater. Dens, needless to say, are precious real estate among arctic foxes, and vixens frequently locate theirs at ancestral sites or appropriate abandoned dens. Early in the season, a vixen excavates a modest nest with a few simple entrances and exits by digging with her pointed forelegs. Later in the arctic summer, after the sun melts the lingering snow and the upper layers of permafrost, she expands her family flat by digging additional exits. Some fox dens are modified to include dozens of entrances and are used by generations of foxes over many decades.

A young arctic fox stands stoically on the tundra, seemingly oblivious to the summer heat and the swarms of bloodsucking blackflies and other insects around its head.

Right: Stealthy as adults, arctic foxes are very curious as kits, and any activity outside the burrow quickly attracts their attention.

Through play, foxes learn valuable hunting skills at an early age. Prey is normally captured with a surprise jump from overhead, and the technique is practiced repeatedly.

The significance of the foxes' instincts struck me with an unusual clarity as I cast my eyes about the Barren Lands. Survival is not something one takes for granted here. Through binoculars, I was able to make out the location of a den just over a mile away. Its telltale markers were a cluster of small shrubs of birch or willow and some sparsely growing light-colored grass near the opening. Tilled into the soil by the vixen's relentless home improvements, the foxes' nutrient-rich droppings produce rare vegetation in an otherwise desolate landscape.

In sharp contrast to the typical constraints of an urban landscape, the Barren Lands have no other defining boundaries anywhere in sight. No trees, shrubs, houses, cars or chimneys interrupt the empty canvas that stops in each direction only where the eye marries heaven and earth. Seemingly endless and possessed by the howling wind—a quality that earned it the name Keewatin, meaning "wind from the North"—the region played havoc with my emotions. It was at once wildly intimidating and coolly seductive, bleak and yet rich with possibility. As we set up camp, I understood that I was confronting the unadorned face of an area which harbors a rich biological heart. Thousands of geese, swans, auks, cranes, shorebirds and songbirds as well as explosive populations of lemmings, mice and hares all live here—and serve as a food source for the foxes I had come to see.

As we wandered less than 100 yards from the tent, we found our den. "Look," said Donald, holding his nose and laughing. "Footprints and fresh droppings." He was right. The strong, pungent smell of urine exposed to warm sunlight hung over the whole area. Undeterred, Donald lay down in front of the hole and whistled into the den. He received a husky barking in reply—proof that the den was occupied. Thanking Donald for his help, I decided to make this spot my headquarters for the next few days.

During three intensive stints of fox watching, I failed to shoot a single frame. Aside from the few breaks I took to relax and stretch my aching muscles, I sat on a little field stool in my hiding place from 5:00 in the morning until after 10:00 each night, staring at the den's main entrance. At that time of year, the sun beat down from morning until late afternoon, and legions of blackflies and other bugs selected my skin to improve the quality of their diets. When I retreated to my tent for a rare break, the vixen chose that moment to dart in and out of her den. Since arctic foxes are thought to be relatively fearless of humans, that troubled me. I wondered whether I should move my blind farther away.

At the end of the third day, however, I spied the beautiful vixen approaching the den with prey dangling from her mouth. Sporting her summertime pelage, the fox wore a coat of short, dark brown fur, her chest and underbelly a creamy buff color. About the size of a large cat (less than three feet long), she had short legs and a bushy tail. Taking advantage of all available cover, she slunk toward the entrance and disappeared into the burrow with a goose chick for dinner. A few minutes later, the fox pups poked their faces out of the various entrances. As I counted 12 fuzzy little kits, I found it almost impossible to remain calm.

No sooner has she returned from a hunt than the mother arctic fox is surrounded by her playful kits. Despite their numbers and their excitable nature, however, the youngsters remain subordinate to their mother.

Hours of wrestling and fighting help hone the skills these young foxes will need as adults when hunting and defending their territory.

104

With a hungry brood waiting at home, the vixen made up to five hunting trips a day to secure food. Snow geese chicks were a favorite—they were either devoured immediately or carried to the "storage cellar" below.

When young arctic foxes first emerge from the den at the end of June, their coats are nearly black. As the summer wears on, however, their fur grows lighter in color until, in late fall, they sport their camouflage winter coats.

Right: Life on water offers a flock of geese only limited protection from a clever fox. Bounding into the middle of a tundra lake, a vixen strikes a chick; the adults can do little but keep at a safe distance and menace the fox with their honking. At this time of year, the geese are unable to fly.

As agile as a cat, this young arctic fox momentarily rears up on its hind legs, watching for its mother to return from the hunt.

Inuksuk
Erected by Inuit many generations ago,
these rock figures served as landmarks
to orient travelers navigating the
wide-open regions of the Barren Lands.

*The leaves of the shrubby Alpine bearberry (**Arctostaphylos alpina**) turn deep red with the first frost, a sign of the northern Indian summer.*

The shelter of a large boulder offers a protected day bed for a young arctic fox in early fall. By mid–September, the fox is approaching 5 months of age and its fur is beginning to turn a lighter shade, the first indication of the dense white winter coat to come.

Bushes of colorful wild blueberries dot the countryside in late summer.

Right: Morning mists drift eerily across the tundra in autumn, silhouetting a lone arctic fox at rest on high ground.

Young foxes are born with a velvety covering of dark brown or gray fur. Helpless, naked and blind at birth, these northern pups develop quickly and are ready for independence in six months. My litter must have already passed the two- or three-week mark. They were eating solid food and venturing outside, where they played with abandon, yipping and snorting at each other with open mouths.

Among arctic foxes, a litter of 12 is an average-sized family. The population cycles of small rodents such as lemmings, which constitute the bulk of the diet for foxes living in this region, are the main factor affecting litter size. The foxes' fecundity waxes and wanes with the food supply available during the spring and summer; as a result, they produce as few as five young in some seasons and as many as 25 in others. As often as five times a day, the vixen brings fresh prey to feed her hungry youngsters, and researchers have counted up to 4,000 lemmings on the menu of a single fox family during the breeding season. Filling those empty little stomachs is a lot of work, and hunting trips last anywhere from half an hour to several hours. When a vixen delivers a large number of pups, an older daughter from an earlier litter sometimes participates in finding food. With the family I was observing, however, I saw a more familiar helper: the male. Approaching to within about 500 yards, he would put down prey and then disappear; the vixen would then pick up the food and carry it to the den. Foxes are thought to be monogamous, and both parents are attentive to the young during these early weeks of life. The male will even provide food for the nursing mother.

At 8 weeks of age, the kits are old enough to follow their parents on hunting expeditions. By the fall, however, when geese and other migratory birds head south, the vixen finds it difficult to keep up with the dietary demands of her young, which are approaching 6 months of age and are nearly adult size. About this time, the family begins to disperse. Typically, the father leaves the group before any other family member. The first winter is hard for the newly independent kits, and only three out of four are likely to survive.

Rich in texture and mood, northern landscapes like these have inspired generations of Canadian artists.

Difficult though the winter may be, the arctic fox has successfully inhabited the Arctic and subarctic regions around the North Pole for approximately two million years, and it comes well prepared for the inhospitable environment. To adapt to snow and bitterly cold temperatures that can plunge to minus 94 degrees F, the arctic fox has developed a number of specialized physical traits. In the early winter, for example, its fur turns lighter in color and gradually becomes more dense. By the time snow covers the ground, the arctic fox boasts a thick, white coat that serves as the insulation of choice among mammals in the region. Its dark eyes and black nose are the only contrast on an all-white body, affording it excellent camouflage protection from the snowy owls and polar bears that prey on it. Its thickly furred paws never get cold, thanks to an

Using a deadly feline-style pounce, an arctic fox makes its headfirst attack on a mouse runway excavated beneath the crusted snow.

elaborate system of countercurrent blood vessels that keep a continuous supply of warm blood flowing through the soft tissue. During active hours, the fox increases its metabolism and maintains its body temperature even when the air is coldest. Conversely, when at rest, it conserves energy with a metabolism that functions at a very low level. Only during the fiercest storms does an arctic fox need to seek shelter.

Outside the breeding season, the arctic fox is a solitary hunter that relies heavily, as do other canids, on its sense of smell. Tracking in a zig-zag pattern, the little fox keeps its nose close to the ground, attempting to pick up the scent of food—mice or lemmings in nests or runways under the snow. The rodents seek shelter under a hard cover of snow that has been formed and compacted by the continuous winds. Such

Right: Licking its lips in satisfaction, an arctic fox emerges from behind a pile of sea ice. Feeding on the meaty leftovers of abandoned bear kills, foxes will follow their carnivorous leaders onto the pack ice for more than 100 miles. In their continuous search for food, foxes can travel up to 300 miles in a single season.

strongholds pose little trouble for the innovative fox, however, which first scratches the hardened surface enough to weaken its structure. Then, leaping almost straight up into the air in a catlike maneuver, it pounces headfirst on top of its unsuspecting prey, sinking shoulder-deep into the snow cover.

Opportunistic in their feeding habits, scavenger foxes search the sea ice for food, taking advantage of the abundant flesh of whale, seal or caribou kills left behind by hunting polar bears. Some foxes have been found 125 miles away from the coast, drifting along on ice floes. Such feasting can be a double-edged undertaking for the foxes, though, which remain prime prey for larger predators such as bears and wolves.

Lady

I will never forget the winter of 1992 on Hudson Bay. It was unusually dry that year, and snow didn't fall until November. More memorable than the weather, though, was the week I spent in the company of two Canadian photographers, trekking across the frozen tundra lakes on the trail of a spectacular arctic fox that we named "Lady."

Rather shy for the first few days, Lady quickly became more social. Eventually, she even came close enough to sniff inquisitively at the base of our camera tripods and along the soles of our shoes. In obvious good health, she wore a flawless plush white coat that, against the crystal-blue sky, made her the model wildlife subject. Throughout the day, we found that when we weren't following Lady, she was following us. It was a nature photographer's paradise.

On one occasion, I lay prone on the ice of a frozen lake and watched through the viewfinder as Lady cautiously approached and stopped in front of the camera's wide-angle lens. Curious about the reflection in the glass, she gently pressed her nose against it. But she quickly lost interest in the inedible piece of equipment and turned and wandered away. I've had many different experiences in my career as a photographer of wild animals, but lying there eye-to-eye with the vixen was indeed a new one.

Lady's fearlessness around the cameras and our little crew may have made her life somewhat unique among arctic foxes, but her death in a hunter's trap a month later was all too familiar. For centuries, foxes have been hunted for their fine fur coats. Today, furriers in Germany, Japan and Italy are among the prime buyers of these luxuriant pelts, and in some arctic regions, any trapper who enjoys the motorized benefits of a snowmobile can set as many as 400 spring traps and snare more than 1,000 foxes in a season. The healthy arctic fox population that annually entertains visitors to Churchill, Manitoba, does not itself seem to be threatened by overhunting, but other less abundant species, such as the snowy owl and gyrfalcon, are innocent victims of the hunt. Caught in traps set for the foxes, they face an agonizing death from exposure to the elements.

A stealthy and equally formidable enemy currently assaulting all arctic ecosystems is pollution. Heavy metals that are released into the natural environment during oil exploration of the ocean floor, such as mercury and barium, as well as PCBs and an astonishing host of pesticides that waft to northern waters from the industrialized temperate zones are all evident in the region's food chain. Contamination at the lowest rung gradually works its way up and into the tissues of belugas, walruses and seals. Though they do not live in the water, carnivores that feed on these aquatic prey species, such as polar bears and arctic foxes, are thereby subjected to the insidious by-products of our civilization—with fatal results.

With its nose to the ground, this elegant arctic fox is always on the lookout for food.

Right: Despite the habitat's extreme temperatures, arctic foxes rarely seek shelter from the cold. They can endure the weather even when the mercury drops to minus 90 degrees F.

The December sun casts a long shadow on a lone arctic hunter.

As spotless as a pedigree show dog, Lady sports a thick, pure white coat that is irresistibly attractive to human hunters. Despite the large number of foxes taken each year, the overall population of this northern canid remains stable.

The tree line marks the southern boundary of the arctic foxes' distribution.

Right: My teeth chattered for 20 minutes as I endured minus-36-degree-F temperatures, waist-deep in a snowdrift, waiting for a three-second sitting with this magnificent fox. Portrait taken, it proceeded on its way.

Polar Bears and Their World
A Short History

The ancient ancestors of today's family of bears appeared about 20 million years ago on the European continent. The first species, known as the dawn bear, was a small animal approximately the size of a fox terrier. From this original ursine root, several intermediate species emerged, including the giant short-faced bear, which lived as recently as 11,000 years ago. Twice the size of today's 800-pound grizzly, the short-faced bear earned a reputation as the most massive carnivorous land mammal the world has ever known.

Modern bears, which are the largest of the carnivores, have radiated into eight species worldwide: brown, American black, polar, sun, sloth, panda, Asiatic black and spectacled. The last descendant to appear in this long evolutionary line is the polar bear. Piecing together the history of this species from fossilized records, researchers believe

Rolling around on the snow, endlessly amused by this discarded tire, an adult polar bear displays the same love of play evident among immature cubs.

that the polar bear came into existence roughly 100,000 years ago, a descendant of brown bears from Siberia which were stranded in the North by the advancing glaciation. (Theories about the close relationship between these two species are supported by the fact that they can crossbreed when in captivity.) Cold though the new habitat may have been, an abundance of high-fat seals and the absence of competition and predation made the transformation possible.

The same characteristics—size, power and fearlessness—that allowed the original Siberian migrants to make the transition to the arctic habitat one million years ago may also help to explain why, as far back as recorded history, humans have revered and found spiritual sustenance in bears. Early in the 20th century, a German archaeologist, for example, uncovered an altar deep within a labyrinth of caves high in the Alps that was adorned with seven bear skulls. Markings at the cave entrance revealed that the excavation was the 75,000-year-old home of a Neanderthal tribe which may have been very familiar with some of the early cave-dwelling bear species. In another cave near Montestan, France, scientists unearthed a clay representation of a bear's torso that was riddled with holes. They speculate that Stone Age hunters covered this mannequin with a real bear's head and pelt for worship during ceremonial rites and dances. Most recently, at an isolated lake in Siberia, Russian biologist Savva Uspenskii found several bear heads that had been carefully arranged as a place of worship. Bear-tooth talismans symbolizing the bear's power and strength were worn by early Cro-Magnon man (c. 12,000 to 5000 B.C.) and are echoed today in similar amulets adorning the necks of many Inuit.

Inuit legends are replete with the spiritual mysteries of the bear. One such tale was brought to the non-Inuit world by anthropologist Franz Boas after he met the residents of Baffin Island in 1883: It is told that an Angakok—an Inuit medicine man—wants to increase his power by gaining mastery over the big bear, which would then become his Tornaq, or secret source of support. To win such loyalty from the bear, the Angakok travels to the end of the known land. There, he calls out to the bears. When a large group of bears gathers around him, the Angakok collapses with fright. If, when he falls to the ground, he lands on his back, the Angakok dies on the spot. If he falls on his face, however, a bear comes forward and offers himself as the medicine man's Tornaq. Whenever the Angakok needs help or faces danger in the future, the bear will intercede on his behalf.

Every friendship has its testing point: When a visiting bear tried to steal food from this sled dog, the hunter became the hunted.

Bear and Dog: An Unusual Friendship

Over the years, the antics of bears have been captured in a number of unforgettable images—cubs or adolescent bears in playful poses and big bears wrestling in the snow or entertaining themselves with unfamiliar objects—but in 1992, visitors to Churchill, Manitoba, witnessed an unlikely relationship between polar bears and some Canadian Eskimo dogs owned by Brian Ladoon.

Ladoon's dog kennel is located a few miles outside Churchill, and for several days, a large white polar bear had been lounging nearby. Friendly and apparently social, this Nanook showed no aggressive behavior; instead, it spent most of its time sleeping behind the cover of a large rock formation.

One of Ladoon's best dogs, a large male named Hudson, was secured by a 30-foot-long leash that was anchored to the ground. From my comfortable vantage point inside a warm car only a few feet away from where the dogs were chained, I could see the bear casually making its way in our direction, stopping occasionally, with nose held high, to sniff the air. Perhaps picking up the dog's scent, the curious bear suddenly turned and started to amble toward Hudson, a move that caused pandemonium among the ranks of the other 39 dogs, which began wildly barking, jerking at their chains and spinning in frantic circles. Hudson, however, calmly stood his ground and began wagging his tail to greet the approaching bear.

More than once, an angry polar bear has been known to kill teams of dogs tethered outside, eliminating the canines one at a time as it made its way along the line. But these two animals did not behave as adversaries. Touching noses, they puzzled over each other's smell, standing so close that either could likewise have tested its teeth. But what we saw, instead, was a fascinating game of trust between two radically unmatched players.

A bear that had been watching the scene from a distance also decided to approach. Was it, too, going to attempt to play with one of the barking dogs? The bear cautiously inched forward and closed in on Barren. In a gesture of complete submission to his new friend, Barren rolled onto his back and stretched out his neck in an effort to nudge the bear's snout with his own. Seemingly stunned by this enthusiastic playmate, the bear tentatively reached its paw forward, as if to test Barren's reaction. Crawling closer, the bear next pinched the dog's skin with its furry snowshoe-sized paw, causing the dog to let out a hoarse

Ancient enemies become fast friends in the relaxed atmosphere of Churchill, Manitoba. Putting aside their ancestral animus, these two played together harmlessly each afternoon for 10 days in a row in 1992.

yelp. As the bear moved within reach, however, Barren showed no fear. Lunging forward, he gently nipped Nanook's tiny ear and immediately found himself wrapped in a friendly bear hug. I could hardly believe what I was seeing. Like two roughhousing kids, the pair tumbled around on the ground for several minutes, allowing me to snap roll after roll of film. After they grew tired, they retreated a safe distance from each other to rest.

In an attempt to explain such atypical behavior, Laury Brouzes of the Department of Natural Resources in Churchill theorizes that the dominant bears might have been flaunting their compatibility with the dogs in the expectation of earning a handout. As if to support that point of view, the bears did indeed linger in the area of the dog compound for long periods, perhaps in the hope of sharing the daily meal of their newfound friends.

Incidents of hostility between bears and dogs, however, are far more common in the Inuit settlements in the North than is the friendly little exchange we observed. In fact, 99 percent of the bears behave quite aggressively toward dogs; many a companion and working dog has lost its life trying in vain to defend its food. In spite of the ancestral rivalry between dogs and bears, though, Ladoon has lost only three of his animals to polar bear attacks in the past 17 years. In two cases, the deaths were accidental; only the third was the result of aggression. Though these bears possess the power to kill easily, the behavior I witnessed suggests that they are much more than simply voracious predators.

Though unequally matched—the bear is 10 times the size of its canine playmate—these two wrestled, hugged and tugged at each other for hours of apparently good-natured fun.

Brian Ladoon,
Man of the North

Canadian Eskimo dog.

Polar Pals
Right: Brian Ladoon with one of his four-legged companions. Before setting out on a dogsled tour, Ladoon dons a parka and trousers made from polar bear skin. Wind-resistant and warm, the outfit is the ultimate in arctic attire.

A well-known painter in northern Canada, Brian Ladoon was born and raised in Churchill, Manitoba. Under the caring guidance of his father, he grew up to be a man whose entire existence—his work, his spirituality and his creativity—is completely integrated with nature. Without any formal training, Ladoon has become a master hunter, trapper, fisher, craftsman and expert breeder of Canadian Eskimo dogs.

According to the Canadian Kennel Club, the Canadian Eskimo dog is the traditional working dog of northern indigenous people; some even argue that it is the oldest breed of domesticated dog in the world. Originally kept 2,000 years ago by the Thule culture, the breed was likely brought to the Canadian Arctic when its masters migrated there from Northeast Asia, near the Bering Sea. Its close connection to its wolf ancestor—a claim commonly made by Inuit—is apparent in the breed's mournful howling.

When the snowmobile began to replace the dogsled as the arctic vehicle of choice in the late 20th century, however, the breed might have faced extinction were it not for the intervention of the Canadian Kennel Club. Fearing the potential demise of one of five recognized truely Canadian dog breeds, the Eskimo Dog Research Foundation selected a few individuals from the North to become the breeding stock of the registered line.

For speed and strength, Eskimo dogs rank somewhere between the Siberian husky and the Alaskan malamute. Generations of adaptation to the unforgiving surroundings, however, have made the dog a hardy arctic specialist. Its naturally oily and waterproof coat, which occurs in a host of canine colors, is composed of a two-inch-thick woolly underlayer covered with six-inch-long guard hairs. The Eskimo dog is big-boned and muscular, and its feet have large, thick pads that are protected with a heavy covering of fur. The compact breed stands two feet high at the shoulder and can easily weigh 100 pounds, and its reputation for loyalty and a good nature is legendary. Exceptionally dedicated to its work, the breed proved invaluable to such early polar explorers as Admiral Robert Edwin Peary and Roald Amundsen. In his journals, Peary paid high honor to his canine team, which "day after day struggled across that awful frozen desert, fighting for their lives and ours; day after day, they worked till the last ounce of work was gone from them, and they fell dead in their tracks without a sound."

While few of today's Eskimo dogs need endure such marathon adventures, most still work at the job for which they have been bred. Ladoon, for example, bought his first dogs in 1976 at the Inuit villages of Hall Beach and Carol Harbour and today uses two teams for sled tours and excursions in the Churchill area. His teams are handsome, strong, well trained and eager to start their working winter from the time the bay ice is thick enough to traverse until it melts at the end of May.

Ladoon's dog compound faces the wind-battered coast of Hudson Bay, and his 40 dogs are leashed on the banks of a nearby small freshwater lake. They live there happily for most of their 11-year life span, requiring very little in the way of protection from the weather. Curled up and covered by their bushy tails, they survive the fiercest snowstorms, suffering little more than a fine dust-

ing of snow that clings to their dense coats. (Their most trying time of the year, in fact, is summer, when the searing sun beats down and hungry mosquitoes, blackflies, sandflies and horseflies torment them.) Ladoon drives a little over seven miles to his dog compound every day to feed, groom and play with the dogs. During the coldest times of the year, when they work the hardest and burn up vast amounts of energy, each dog consumes between 5 and 10 pounds of high-fat, high-protein food daily.

Although it is only one facet of Ladoon's life here on Hudson Bay, his love of and devotion to his family of dogs and the tireless work that they gladly give in return are, I have learned, emblematic of the

Under the power of a team of 11 sled dogs, Ladoon's homemade komatik is whisked easily across the frozen Churchill River. The northern chariot of choice, the dogsled is an efficient mode of transportation for week-long hunting trips across the icy snow-covered terrain.

Right: A traditional Inuit igloo, here illuminated from the inside, provides the perfect temporary refuge from the numbingly cold nights.

goodness in the souls of people from the North. They live harmoniously with the land and with each other, ever willing to help a friend in need.

The Tour

One year in late winter, Ladoon and I made arrangements to tour the countryside surrounding Churchill by dogsled. When we met at the kennel and I first spotted Ladoon, he looked like a true man of the North. He had donned a jacket and pants made from polar bear fur and gloves and shoes made of sealskin. A seasoned outdoorsman, Ladoon knows how to keep warm, and the thick homemade clothes provide him with impenetrable protection against the cold.

Harnessed in their towing gear, 11 dogs were connected to a long rope. The lead dog took up his position at the front, while five pairs fell in line behind. The entire team was secured by a safety line to the 15-foot-long sled, which Ladoon made himself. Known to Inuit as a komatik, the ample sled is covered with caribou skin, which provides a comfortable cushion during long hours on the snow.

As soon as Ladoon loosened the safety line, the dogs eagerly dashed off. Instinctively, they headed for Hudson Bay, threading their way between huge blue- and green-tinted blocks of compressed ice that were strewn haphazardly across its frozen surface. After charging a few hundred yards at full throttle, the team slowed to a steady trot. Ladoon varied his trip by sometimes standing on the back of the sled and sometimes running alongside, yelling commands to the obedient team. "Yak-yak-yak," he cried to turn left, "Gee-gee-gee" to turn right. Proud of his team's skill, he occasionally laughed with delight as the komatik skated silently over the glittering ground. Despite the cold, our two-hour trip flew by. Back at the kennel, as I watched the dogs feast on their well-deserved meal, I understood that my most recent arctic adventure had been more than a quaint excursion down memory lane. Perhaps by virtue of its authenticity—but more likely because of its simplicity—this trip by sled had offered me my most intimate view to date of the splendor of the Arctic.

Security
Boris Oszurkievicz uses spiked boards across the entranceway and windows of his house to discourage visits from the foraging King of the North. As an added measure of protection, he sleeps with his rifle close at hand.

Warning signs mark unsafe areas on the outskirts of town.

Until the clampdown on vagrant bears a few years ago, polar bears were a common sight at the Churchill garbage dump. In their single-minded search for food, rummaging bears would sift through the debris, licking food-scented containers and often sustaining injuries from broken glass or from aluminum cans that could become jammed between their teeth and gums. In an attempt to discourage this behavior, wildlife officers now tranquilize all ursine garbage offenders and temporarily incarcerate them.

Polar Bear Alert

Despite everything I've learned about polar bears from my travels with experienced researchers, I have still, on occasion, found myself in alarming proximity to the odd unruly animal. In 1989, for instance, I was parked in a truck near Brian Ladoon's kennel, observing a gang of seven bears that had been milling about for several hours—not an unusual circumstance. An older bear with singed fur on its head slowly approached the vehicle, circled it and then stood up on its hind legs in

Tranquilizer darts for the narcotic gun.

search of food on the truck bed. Finding nothing edible, the creature settled for mischief instead, moving forward to the hood of the truck, where it dropped out of sight. Suddenly, the truck began to rock back and forth, and I spotted my white-coated friend at one of the front wheels, tugging with all its might. Before I could start the engine to scare the bear off, it had chomped the tire flat with its large flesh-tearing teeth. In a bit of a panic, I wrenched the key in the ignition, put the truck in gear and pulled away, thumping overland on a flat tire and barely making it to the safety of the main road, where I was able to put on the spare.

Comical though this memory is now, it was a sobering reminder that polar bears deserve respect. Between the 1960s and the early 1980s, Churchill was an increasingly popular destination for *Ursus maritimus*, and a dispute about human versus polar bear rights became a heated local topic. Residents had always tolerated the bears, but unwanted encounters between the townsfolk and the hungry, intimidating transients were on the rise. Polar bears strolled through Churchill during the daytime. One year, for example, as many as 40 bears were counted at the town's garbage dump and more than 60 were spotted roaming near houses. Residents had to be careful when they were out on the street (especially at night), for fear of inadvertently cornering a bear in an alley. Sometimes, bears even broke into homes and ransacked them in search of food.

In 1969, Manitoba's Department of Natural Resources established the Polar Bear Control Program. Increased vigilance, reinforced doors and nail-studded boards became part of a grass roots deterrent program within Churchill. During October and November, nervous residents outside the main town went to bed with rifles close at hand, because bears were breaking into homes and surprising people as they slept. Two serious bear-human encounters in the early 1980s—one was a fatal incident between a hungry bear and an intoxicated man—changed the town's long-standing bear-tolerant attitudes. Especially vocal were newcomers to town, who advocated zero tolerance for so-called nuisance bears, recommending that the interlopers be shot on sight.

Flying in the face of these antibear sentiments are statistics that clearly make an argument for the bears. They show that the risk of being killed by a polar bear in the Far North is far less than the risk of being struck by lightning, dying from a bee sting or being killed in a train crash. A University of Calgary study examined 381 incidents involving bears and humans between 1965 and 1985 and found that 353 of them were harmless and 28 involved injury, 8 of which were deadly for humans. In 251 of the cases, in fact, the bears were killed. Bears are not wanton man-eaters; in each of these cases, the people were carry-

ing food, making them obvious targets for a hungry bear.

Those who wave the banner of deadly force temporarily forget what many unfortunate victims consider too late: it is humans who are the trespassers in what has been, for thousands of years, a traditional wild-bear habitat. From the burgeoning industry of wilderness adventures that place us in wildlife habitat to geological surveys and resource extraction that sometimes occur smack-dab in the middle of the polar bears' migratory routes, humans have made it their business to put themselves in close proximity to these creatures, thus bringing about the increase in bear-human contact. And yet for a long time, we expected bears to pay the

consequences for such contact with their lives. The most clearheaded views on the issue came from longtime Churchill residents themselves, who argued that you shouldn't live in Churchill if you are not willing to respect the presence of the polar bears for a few weeks each year.

By 1984, the vigilance campaign was officially renamed the Polar Bear Alert. It was a reflection of the changing attitudes toward the bears, I suppose, possibly the result of Churchill's increased popularity as a tourist retreat and of new information gleaned from research that the Canadian Wildlife Service had been conducting since the 1960s. In the hope of increasing the safety of both residents and bears, the emphasis of the Alert program is on awareness. Signs around town mark unsafe areas, and people of all ages are educated in how to reduce opportunities for bear contact. Today, bears caught regularly hanging around the dump are incarcerated at the Polar Bear Compound until freeze-up. Hard-core garbage groupies and otherwise hostile individuals are tranquilized and shipped hundreds of miles up the coast.

Despite the presence of the occasional nuisance bear in town, Churchill is unique because of its bears. It is the only venue in the entire world where people can see these magnificent creatures up close. Whether you choose to live or to travel in the North, it is important to keep in mind who the interloper is and to act accordingly. Much like the cold climate, these creatures are an inherent part of life in the North—and I suspect no one has ever filed a complaint with the authorities asking that something be done about the weather.

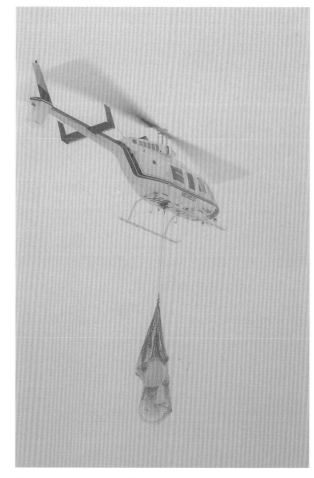

Drugged bears are airlifted to the North Knife River by helicopter, where they are set free. After about two hours, the bears wake up and continue their trip to the coast in anticipation of the imminent early-winter freeze.

Left: As soon as there is sufficient ice on Hudson Bay, bears that have been confined in the Polar Bear Compound are transported to the coast and released.

Interview with Laury Brouzes of the Department of Natural Resources in Churchill, Manitoba, about the Polar Bear Alert, March 18, 1993.

Q: During October and November, how many polar bears wander between Cape Churchill and the town of Churchill?

A: About 400 to 500 bears are in the region, but only 20 percent at most ever venture into town.

Q: How long has the Polar Bear Alert been active?

A: It was established in 1969 but underwent a change in its form following some serious incidents in 1983, including the death of one man.

Q: What does the Polar Bear Alert do?

A: Our first priority is to protect people and their property. In doing that, however, we also want to protect the polar bears from the consequences of contact with humans. Part of the mandate of the new program was to define areas that are strictly off limits to the bears. As a result, we have set a no-bear radius of four to five miles around the town—excluding the shores of Hudson Bay. Any bear that violates this "control zone" is immediately removed.

Q: How is the bear removed?

A: Initially, we try to scare the bear out of town using the sirens on our trucks or cracker shells fired from a shotgun. If that doesn't work, we have three methods for capturing the bear. The first is known as the culvert trap, which is simply a large section of sewer pipe with a strong grid at the rear, where we attach bait to entice the bear inside. Once the bear enters the pipe, a trapdoor at the front swings closed. The second method is a simple rope trap that snags the bear by the leg. When all else fails, we use a tranquilizer gun.

Q: What happens to the bears you catch?

A: Bears caught in culvert traps and those which we have to sedate are brought to D20, a building constructed in 1982 that serves as the Polar Bear Compound.

Q: How long do the bears stay there?

A: Individuals and families that are picked up have typically been kept in the cells for two to six weeks. In the future, however, there will be no more family

cells. As long as Hudson Bay is not covered with ice, we plan to airlift family groups by helicopter to the North Knife River and release them. If the bay ice has already developed, the bears will be transported to the coast by truck and turned loose.

Q: What is the reaction of the townspeople to your work?

A: When we polled the people after last year's bear season, the opinions were favorable. The residents seem satisfied that we are protecting them and their property and keeping the town free of polar bears. I think we've been successful.

Q: Have there been any particularly persistent polar bears?

A: We caught 62 bears last year, and very early in the season—about September, I think—we received a call on the Polar Bear Alert line informing us that a bear was in town. When we found him, we used our deterrent methods to scare him out of town, staying on his trail until he swam into Hudson Bay. Despite our efforts, however, he returned, and for two days, we couldn't catch him, even though we received more than 10 phone calls alerting us to his whereabouts. We finally decided to sedate him and lock him up, but unfortunately, he had learned to recognize our truck. He didn't run from other vehicles; in fact, he pressed his nose against their windows. But whenever we approached, he ran off, traveling up to 30 miles per hour to get away. We never had a chance to get a good shot.

Finally, on the third night, someone notified us that the bear was trapped in a garage. We had to blind him temporarily using a million-candlepower spotlight so that he wouldn't recognize the truck. Then I shot him with a tranquilizer dart, and he woke up in the compound. That fellow was a bad bear. He was 7 years old and weighed over 750 pounds. Three years earlier, he had broken into and demolished the depot of a regional airline, devouring food that was scheduled to be airlifted north.

The Polar Bear: An Economic Factor

The number of polar bears worldwide is estimated to be between 20,000 and 30,000, with about 15,000 of these inhabiting Canadian wilderness.

For the indigenous hunters of northern Canada and Alaska, the polar bear, like the caribou and the seal, is not a mere trophy but is a plentiful source of fur, clothing and food, which explains why some of the several hundred polar bears killed annually are taken in Canada.

During the 1980s, a polar bear skin commanded a tidy sum that ranged from $500 to $3,000 (Cdn). While the domestic hunt of polar bears is forbidden in the province of Manitoba, 52 hunting licenses (allowing only 52 bears to be taken) are issued among the communities

 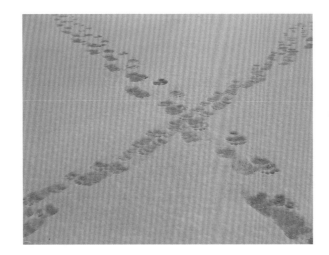 

Photo: Fritz Pölking

Bear tracks and human tracks crisscross in the snow near Churchill. Tundra buggies and buses full of tourists drive to the east side of Churchill to view the polar bears in their natural habitat. In some cases, the bears make a concerted effort to greet the tourists.

of the Northwest Territories, some of which are just north of the provincial boundaries. A number of these permits are, at the community's discretion, made available to foreign sport hunters. These hunters pay tens of thousands of dollars for the privilege of hunting Nanook, pumping money into the economy of the Northwest Territories and stimulating the local demand for Inuit guides and services.

Parked near the Hudson Bay coast during the polar bear season, a mobile hotel offers three-day accommodations for visiting photographers, filmmakers, writers and tourists who want to enjoy hours of close-up observation of these fascinating mammals.

A Tourist Visit to the Polar Bears

One frosty October morning, I was among a group of excited tourists on its way to see the polar bears up close at Cape Churchill. Securely wrapped in thick parkas and laden with cameras, binoculars and box lunches, we stamped our cold feet and anxiously waited for a bus to pick us up at the Polar Inn and take us to the polar bears' tundra playground, nine miles outside of town.

As we made our way to the outskirts of Churchill, the sun's circular red edge peeked above the eastern horizon and cast a warm morning glow across the harsh land. When we arrived at our rendezvous spot—called "the tundra parking lot"—big all-terrain buses were standing by to carry us over the rocky landscape to our destination. Our driver and guide was Dwight Allen, who was also the manager of our hotel. Having grown up in Churchill, Dwight proved an excellent tour leader, very familiar with the town history, the outdoors and the 90-minute trip that lay ahead. As we bounced over a well-traveled mud path, negotiating puddles and ice sludge and crossing shallow lakes, the bus rarely made it out of low gear. Dwight patiently navigated the unpredictable terrain, cautiously avoiding the large and unyielding boulders that scarcely broke the surface of the ground but could potentially send the bus violently careening from side to side.

One hour into the trip, we passed First Tower, a wooden structure erected by the military during the 1970s. As we closed in on the coast, each of us fantasized about being the first to see a bear. The suspense was palpable. "There's one!" shouted an American woman. "Over there, on the other side of the lake." Dwight made his approach, cutting the engine when we were within 200 yards of the bear. "We'll let him come to us," he explained. "Bear watching takes time and patience."

Indeed. The bear moved slowly toward us, pausing every few steps to look from side to side. It was a magnificent sight. The light of the morning sun cast a colored halo around his spotless coat, and his hot breath rose visibly in the frigid air. He held his nose high, sniffing and trying to pick up our scent. Judging from the size and shape of his head and body, this fellow was probably 15 years old and weighed over 1,000 pounds. But he was by no means the biggest of them all. A mature male polar bear can weigh over 1,300 pounds, measure 4 feet high at the shoulder and stand 10 feet tall on his hind legs.

Our cameras were operating at full speed. Everybody wanted to take the photograph or video of a lifetime. Before the polar bear bug was able to overwhelm our judgment, however, Dwight cautioned us not to rest our elbows on the window ledges. "Another bear could come from underneath the vehicle," he warned, "and before you'd see him, he could sever your arm muscles with a single swipe of his paw." Apparently, an American photographer was injured in just this fashion in 1987.

By the time our bear reached the bus and stood up to greet us, I realized that I had underestimated his stature. As he pressed his nose against the window and his heavy breathing fogged the glass, I could tell that he was at least 10 feet tall. Finding nothing edible within reach, he demonstrated his brute power by rocking the bus back and forth as if it were a tippy canoe. But when Dwight started the engine, our ursine visitor dashed off. Recovering from the momentary jolt of fear that the bear's unexpected show of strength had inspired, we all relaxed and took a well-deserved break to change film and to savor our cheese sandwiches, which tasted like ambrosia in the cold, clear air.

After lunch, we ventured out to Gordon Point, a neck of land extending into Hudson Bay, where other buses and four big tundra buggies had gathered to watch a bear family of three. As we cautiously drew near, we saw a large female and her twin cubs lying in the grass. In puzzled response to the approaching big-wheeled vehicles, the twins took turns clambering onto their mother's back.

The endless antics of this photogenic threesome might have kept our attention all afternoon, but by 2 o'clock, the already heavy cloud cover was worsening by the minute. The dull gray-on-gray sky prevented our taking any more photographs, so we decided to return to town, hoping to arrive before dark. All the vehicles formed a convoy that inched along the tundra road, swinging from side to side across its uneven surface. It was late when we arrived, and we were all cold and hungry, but the stories that we shared and would take back to our friends and families left us enormously satisfied.

One day at the height of the polar bear season, I counted 37 bears in the immediate vicinity of the rolling hotel, which is a popular departure point for the bears on their winter migration.

Peak Season

The best time of year to watch polar bears is from October 10 through the first week in November. But just as there are no set rules governing the tempestuous northern weather, there are none for the bears either. The polar bear season relies on the travel schedule of the bears themselves as they make their way to the coast. There may be no bears in early October, or they may have left long before early November; just as unpredictably, the season may extend well into December. Regardless of the migration pattern in an individual year, all tour organizers stop offering trips to the tundra by the end of the first week of November.

One of the more novel tour operations in Churchill is the brainchild of Len Smith. An innovative mechanic, Smith built his first tundra buggy in 1979. It was the tundra vehicle of choice for visiting journalists and filmmakers for years. Its unique look, efficiency and durability when driven over the rugged terrain earned the buggy a celebrity status of its own, and it remains the basis of Smith's current business, Tundra Buggy Tours Ltd.—the biggest tour operation in Churchill.

During the peak weeks of the bear-watching season, Smith's company also offers a hotel-on-wheels at the Hudson Bay coast. Made up of five interconnected vehicles, the rolling hotel provides food and lodging to visitors and comes fully equipped with a lounge and sleeping quarters. Photographers especially enjoy the coach's 12-foot-high rear platform, which makes an ideal perch for viewing the dozens of bears attracted by the aromas from the mobile hotel's kitchen. On one occasion, I counted 37 bears milling about. I remember thinking that it was a complete reversal of roles from a modern-day zoo—in this case, the humans were in the cage, while the bears roamed freely about.

Up to 10,000 tourists flock to Churchill each year to watch the polar bears and explore the tundra aboard special buggies and buses.

Custom tundra vans, available for professional photographers from White Bear Pro Photo Tours, offer an excellent base from which to photograph regional wildlife.

A mini-bus from Wilderness Encounter takes curious onlookers to see families of bears, which never seem to tire of human visitors.

A King Without a Realm?

It took 20 million years of gradual natural adaptation to the unique arctic surroundings for the polar bear to evolve into the species we now know. These days, however, I wonder whether this King of the Arctic will still be around a hundred years hence.

In the early 1970s, there were alarming signs of threats against Nanook. The polar bear was classified "endangered," a consequence of intense and uncontrolled hunting. In 1976, an international agreement on endangered species was drawn up to protect the polar bears from an abrupt demise. It designated the polar bear and its habitat as being at risk and resulted in a total ban on bear hunting. The Arctic's five bordering nations—Canada, the United States, Denmark, Norway and the former U.S.S.R.—signed the treaty. While Canada has since lifted this ban and now manages a strictly regulated hunt, Russia continues to enforce it. Canada also plans to establish a federal parkland stretching from Cape Churchill to York Factory, where polar bears and their young will be protected.

The cause of polar bear rights has received a tremendous boost from tourism. In a few short years, the bears have graduated from being pests and mischief-makers in the public perception to becoming the backbone of a local economy that supports both an airline and a wildlife-tour industry, as well as several hotels and restaurants. The 10,000 tourists who visit Churchill each year to see the bears contribute between $1 million and $1.5 million (Cdn) to the local economy. Another source of polar bear promotion has come from the core of field researchers who study the bears' behavior and monitor their populations. Finally, photographers, writers and filmmakers travel to Churchill from all over the world to gather background information for books, periodicals, magazines and documentary films. The current popularity of polar bears and the increasing number of people who are bitten by the polar bear bug may be just what it takes to fuel the movement to protect the bears and the other species that inhabit the Arctic region.

The Endangered Kingdom

At one time, hunting represented the most imminent danger to *Ursus maritimus*. Today, however, this threat has been replaced by a more insidious condition: pollution of the air, oceans and land where these bears live.

Resource extraction, such as drilling for oil and mining in the Arctic, and the associated increased traffic pose one of the biggest dangers to arctic habitats. This assault is augmented by a list of industrial chemicals—PCBs, dioxin, DDT, chlordane, lindane and other toxic ingredients from fertilizers and herbicides—that are carried 2,500 miles by rivers, winds and ocean currents to the Arctic from industrial regions to the south.

Once there, these pollutants wreak havoc with the survival rates of each species when they enter the water column and gradually work their way up the food chain. (Researchers estimate that levels of contamination are intensified by a factor of 10 with each step up.) A study by the Canadian Atmospheric Environment Service, for example, revealed traces of pollutants in the air, water and snow and ultimately discovered concentrations in the fatty tissues of large mammals that sit at the top of the food chain, such as belugas and polar bears.

While this exponential increase in toxicity may sound especially perilous for Nanook—the leading polar predator—it is equally troubling for humans. Though pollution of the Arctic and its species may be an out-of-sight, out-of-mind issue for temperate-zone inhabitants, who consider themselves a distant link in the Earth's food chain, it is a danger faced on a daily basis by modern Inuit, whose subsistence fare comes from fish, seals and whale meat.

Impressions of Winter

Northern Lights: A Symphony of Eternity

The endless expanse of the clear night sky overhead one icy arctic February evening made me feel small and humble. Standing knee-deep in snow beneath the cathedral dome of midnight-blue accented with twinkling lights, I had endured three hours of numbing minus-36-degree-F cold in the hope of witnessing one of nature's most spectacular celestial events: the northern lights, or aurora borealis.

Near midnight, the sky flickered in the east. A transparent green spot in the distance raced toward me, growing in size. It was dragging a long, sweeping tail whose luminous rays were woven together in a fluttering display. From one second to the next, this half-coiled greenish yellow snake filled the sky, and its undulating palette warmed the snowy landscape with a chartreuse glow. The aurora slithered west, releasing strands of light in serpentine spasms as I stood frozen in my tracks. My pounding heart, rising body temperature and frost-covered eyeglass lenses, however, betrayed my irrepressible elation at the sight of this otherworldly spectacle.

At 1:30 a.m., the molten-orange moon peeked above the horizon, and another auroral wave billowed across the sky. Occasionally, like diaphanous curtains, the sheaths of light parted and ejected an illuminated dust. Then they passed slowly in front of the glorious moon, fading as they traveled west.

Suddenly, however, the aurora erupted straight overhead, releasing bright red and purple needles that clustered in colorful bundles. The light beams surrounded me, and I felt as if I were in the middle of a spinning carousel. The "Symphony of Eternity," as Norwegian polar explorer Fridtjof Nansen called it, danced about me, its rays and beams releasing green, amber, purple and red light. Though hundreds of miles apart, the shafts appeared to converge overhead at the magnetic zenith of this endless polar sky. I was witnessing a coronal aurora, an optical illusion in which these true parallel lines of light appear to touch in infinity. An erupting corona, such as this one, is a breathtaking display: pulsating sheets of light reflect off the tundra snow and ignite the trees and rocks in their fluorescent glow.

At its peak, the radiant extravaganza lasted only a few minutes. Even after it faded, however, a lingering thin white veil resonated with the memory of the miraculous aurora that had come before. At this moment, I recalled the spartan eloquence of polar explorer Robert Scott as he described his first encounter with this celestial event: "It is impossible to view these phenomena without standing in awe."

The northern lights.

Undulating northern lights settle like a veil in front of the rising moon.

Northern lights over a wilderness hut.

Myth

People have pondered the origin of the northern lights for centuries. In the lore of aboriginal northern cultures, in particular, myths and legends abound about the source of the awe-inspiring auroral displays. In one historic fable of the Earth's creation, the Algonquin people of central and eastern Canada tell how Nanabozo, a mythological hero, creates Earth and humans. Before he continues on his travels to the northern lands, however, Nanabozo promises always to watch over his people. As a sign of his presence, he periodically kindles giant flames, whose reflections light up the skies. (Other indigenous people in eastern Canada believed that the northern lights were caused by departed ancestors dancing before the Great Spirit.)

For Inuit of northern Canada, who have enjoyed some of the most frequent and intense displays, the aurora was thought to be produced when the medicine man frolicked with the sky people. In this tale, the medicine man falls into a trance from drumming and singing and rises from his igloo into heaven, where he meets the spirits of his ancestors. He is invited to join in a kind of soccer game played with walrus skulls. Refusing to join in at first, he eventually gives one skull a mighty kick. As it flies through the air, flickering sparks from its surface create the northern lights.

Romantic myths are no more fantastic than some of the earliest "scientific" explanations for the phenomenon. The Vikings, for example, believed that the aurora was the burning rim of the Earth itself, while European and North American settlers speculated that the snow and ice soaked up the summer's midnight sun, then later released the stored light during the perpetually dark winter months. Perhaps the most exotic of all such theories came from Jonas Ramus, a Norwegian priest who claimed in 1707 that a colossal source of energy—stored in a cavern deep beneath Greenland—periodically erupted, releasing searing steam and gases which produced the aurora.

The color radiates from an aurora corona.

156

What Causes the Aurora Borealis?

The northern lights originate with eruptions on the sun. Their visible light and color are created by solar-energy particles striking gas particles in the ionosphere, located between 300 and 620 miles above the Earth's surface. A steady stream of these particles, which comprise positive and negative electrical charges, radiates from the sun at approximately 600 miles per second, in what is known as the solar wind. (Variable in intensity, the solar wind increases every 11 years in concert with sunspot activity on the surface of the sun.) After traveling through space for about a day, the charged particles of the solar wind strike the Earth's magnetosphere, accelerating along the lines of the magnetic field toward the geomagnetic poles. At these points, the solar particles bombard the Earth's atmosphere, and the nitrogen and oxygen gases in the atmosphere begin to glow.

When the energy particles strike nitrogen at high altitudes, the northern lights glow blue or purple. Nitrogen at low altitudes appears red. When the particles strike oxygen, the light produced has a greenish hue, except at altitudes above 155 miles, where oxygen gas glows bright red.

Boasting hundreds of millions of kilowatts—more electrical energy than the combined power generated by all the countries of the world—the solar wind draws on a mere 4 percent of its power to create the dazzling visible light. The remaining energy is released as heat, which generates storms in the upper atmosphere and produces a broad spectrum of harmless radiation.

Strong solar winds and the resulting high-energy northern lights frequently disturb the Earth's magnetic field, however, interfering with military communications networks, air-traffic-control signals and satellite-management installations. The electrical fallout has also been known to cause problems on the ground, ranging from corrosion on the Alaskan pipelines to a severe breakdown of Quebec's electricity supply. On March 13, 1989, a sudden electrical surge—estimated at one billion volts—overloaded that province's power system, and its major cities were shrouded in darkness. While this electromagnetic curtain fell over eastern Canada, North America and most of Europe were treated to a lively display of northern lights.

Fourteen months of observation by the Swedish Viking satellite have uncovered new secrets about the enigmatic northern lights. By studying 45,000 pictures relayed back to Earth via the Canadian-made ultraviolet imager, researchers learned that the northern lights can change size

rapidly and can move quickly. Some oval-shaped displays measured 2,500 miles in diameter, while others covered an area of nearly 400,000 square miles. From photographs taken during the spring, scientists learned that auroras seen at night also occur during the day, although they are not discernible to the naked eye.

But neither scientific explanation nor mystic tales can equal the wonder of experiencing the northern lights firsthand on a bitterly cold arctic night.

This display of northern lights ascends like a spirit behind an A-frame house.

Right: A band of northern lights dances over the tundra like a genie released from a bottle.

An aurora appears to rotate in a chartreuse spiral over the flat landscape.

Sun dogs and a halo ring glow on the dark winter horizon.

Hoarfrost and sunlight turn blades of fine grass into spiked pink crystals.

Light from the rising sun reflects against the contours of a snowdrift, transforming it into a luminous abstract sculpture.

Snowdrifts: Nature's Sculptures

For three days one February, a snowstorm raged through Churchill, paralyzing the town. With peak gales reaching 48 miles per hour and outside temperatures sinking to minus 22 degrees F, the local television station issued a warning that the wind-chill factor was 2600—the ambient equivalent of about minus 90 degrees F.

Every step outside on such bone-chilling days produces aches and pains that are only exaggerated by the futility of trying to move about in the raging whiteout. There is no point of reference to help keep you oriented—fixed landmarks, such as buildings and cars, are visible for mere seconds in the frosty vortex.

The Wind Chill Factor

Established by U.S. researchers during an expedition to Antarctica in 1939, the wind chill factor is a theoretical value that provides a measurement of the cooling effect of the air based on the relationship between temperature and wind speed. For humans, the wind chill factor is a more illuminating measure of cold than the simple ambient temperature, because it accurately reflects the effects of the increasing sensation of cold as the body loses heat. Wind chill can be expressed on a variety of scales, such as degrees Celsius or, as in the chart at top right, watts per square meter:

1400 = Outside activities are uncomfortable, even if the sun is shining.

1600 = Unprotected parts of the body will experience frostbite, depending on the degree of physical activity and the warmth of the sun.

2300 = Skiing and hiking can be dangerous. Unprotected facial skin will freeze in less than one minute.

2700 = Any unprotected skin will freeze in less than one minute.

Wind Chill

Air temp. (°C)	No wind	Wind speed (km/h)						
		10	20	30	40	50	60	70
0	800	900	1100	1200	1300	1300	1300	1400
-5	900	1100	1200	1300	1400	1500	1500	1600
-10	1000	1200	1400	1500	1600	1700	1700	1800
-15	1200	1400	1600	1700	1800	1900	1900	2000
-20	1300	1500	1700	1900	2000	2100	2100	2200
-25	1400	1600	1900	2000	2200	2300	2300	2400
-30	1500	1800	2100	2300	2400	2500	2500	2600
-35	1600	1900	2300	2500	2600	2700	2700	2800
-40	1800	2100	2400	2600	2800	2900	2900	3000

Influence of Wind Chill Factor on the Sensed Temperature

Air temp. (°C)	Wind speed (km/h)								
	3	0	-3	-9	-15	-21	-27	-33	-39
0	19	17	16	13	10	7	5	2	-1
11	-1	-4	-7	-14	-21	-28	-34	-41	-48
22	-6	-10	-14	-22	-30	-38	-46	-54	-62
33	-10	-14	-18	-27	-35	-44	-53	-61	-70
44	-12	-17	-21	-30	-39	-48	-57	-66	-75
55	-14	-18	-23	-32	-41	-51	-60	-69	-79
64	-14	-19	-24	-33	-43	-52	-62	-71	-81
75	-15	-20	-25	-34	-44	-53	-63	-73	-82
87	-15	-20	-25	-35	-44	-54	-63	-73	-83

By early morning, however, the world was transformed. The storm had died down, and sunlight, low on the horizon, washed the snow-blown landscape in a palette of warm tones. As the sky overhead brightened, thousands of glistening snowflakes filled the air. They clung to the remnants of summer grasses and settled in artistic shapes at the lee side of rocks, trees and houses. No sculptor could have been more imaginative.

Snow crystals, wind and light combined to create magnificently colored sculptures that extended horizontally, like peaks of meringue, unsupported by their substrate. Where the sun spilled light over the snow, a multihued scene of orange-red forms was dramatically highlighted by deep blue shadows.

Viewing a drift from an angle, I could see ice crystals blowing across the upper edge and falling gently, like powdered sugar, to form a new shape below. Such endless sifting of windswept crystals creates huge white walls. Originally hexagonal snowflakes, these crystals have been blown across the tundra until collisions with rocks, trees and branches have shattered their original symmetry, reducing them to tiny ice needles one millimeter or less in length. Pressure from the mighty northern wind then packs the crystals into dense drifts of unexpected structural stability. The density of a typical drift, for instance, measures about 25 pounds per cubic foot. By comparison, freshly fallen snow has a density of about one pound per cubic foot.

After enduring such a storm, I often marvel at nature's ability to breathe life back into a land that has been numbed by countless wintry onslaughts. But as I absorb the beauty of the sculpted drifts and the elegance with which they afford insulated runways for lemmings, mice and other rodents, I am reminded in an instant how each strand of the arctic's elaborate tapestry—the climate, the wildlife, the landscape and the people—makes an integral contribution to the unique life of the North.

Full moon rising over the tundra.

Biography

Norbert Rosing: Born 1953.

HOME: Grafrath, Germany (near Munich).

Since 1988, Rosing has been a frequent visitor to the coastal region of Hudson Bay in Canada, where he has photographed the natural wonders of the land and its subarctic fauna. Rosing is also a dedicated photographer of African wildlife, old-growth forests, wildlife reserves and national parks in eastern Germany.

PERSONAL DATA:

1984: Member of the German Association of Wildlife Photographers.

1987: Kodak Nature Photography Grant.

1989, 1990, 1991, 1993: Prizes, awards and honorable mentions in the BBC Wildlife Photographer-of-the-Year Competition.

1990: First Prize for Humor at the World Press Photo Competition in Amsterdam.

FREQUENT CONTRIBUTOR TO MAGAZINES AND BOOKS:

Oasis (Italy), *National Geographic* (United States), *Grande Reportage* (France), *Bunte*, Fotografie draußen (Germany).

PHOTOGRAPHIC EXHIBITIONS:

German Museum for Hunting and Fishing in Munich; Zoological Museum in Kiel; East Prussian Museum in Lüneburg; Hunting and Fishing Museum Schloß Wolfstein in Bavaria.

1992: Contributed 184 pictures for *Unbekanntes Deutschland* (The Unknown Germany), published by Tomus Verlag, Munich.

1993: *Geparde* (Hunting Leopards) with Fritz Pölking, published by Tecklenborg Verlag, Steinfurt.

EQUIPMENT: Leica cameras and lenses.

Excursions Into Photography

On Wildlife Photography

Only a few places on Earth offer as rich a diversity of scenes that can be "painted" with a camera as does the Arctic. Setting aside the challenges of the climate—having to handle equipment at minus 22 degrees F, for instance—late fall, winter and early spring offer dramatic opportunities for capturing the soft, dreamlike texture of reddish-tinged light. Gradual changes in the light's intensity and color from horizon to horizon add a certain mystique to this part of the world.

Standing in the middle of the northern night with its myriad stars above, I am always awestruck at the magic of the aurora borealis caressing the velvety dark skies. Like a giant orange ball, the full moon rises above the horizon with an exceptional purity and beauty. While a painter might reach for a palette and brush, incorporating his own imagination, I must engrave these natural miracles on a piece of celluloid.

I find that my education never ends, and I am constantly pushing myself to learn more. Familiarity with one's equipment and its idiosyncrasies is essential, as is training one's visual perception and imagination, extensive study of one's subject and an ever-broadening knowledge of photographic techniques, which comes from reading books and magazines, visiting art and photography exhibits and sharing information with other photographers and nature lovers.

Just before I press the shutter-release button, I concentrate solely on the image in the viewfinder. Closing my ears to surrounding noises, such as chattering birds or the wind, I ask myself: What is the message of the picture before my eyes? Will the casual observer understand what I am seeing at this very moment? Dedicated consideration of such questions is the key to creating good photographs and has helped me become an inspired and satisfied "painter with a camera."

Following the presentation of the R6, I switched to the Leica "R" System. I needed a camera system that could handle the challenges of the harsh arctic environment. Light conditions can be extremely difficult, and I have faced them all: white subjects on a white background, excessive backlight and glare and long, deep shadows. The optical and mechanical features of the lenses are of the utmost importance in resolving such problems. The rugged and purely mechanical R6 and R6.2 camera housings provide the photographer with all the essential elements: a precise exposure-time selector, a ring for focal-length settings, a brilliant viewfinder, a preselected mirror release and the advantage of being able to work without batteries.

I have been asked many times why I stick with my camera system when there are so many faster "high-tech" options. The answer is simple: My camera is a mechanical workhorse, and the technical and artistic skill it demands will always yield superior images. Also, I am very familiar with this type of system, and that additional ease allows me to take better shots.

Whether your camera system is the cheapest or the most expensive, however, nearly all your pictures will be fuzzy and out of focus if you don't use a tripod. Long before you invest in more expensive lenses, you should acquire a sturdy tripod and see for yourself how the quality of your photographs will improve. Although it can take up to 20 minutes to position the tripod, select and compose the picture and then press the release, the result is indeed worthwhile, as I hope the photographs in this book will attest.

When photographing landscapes and other subjects at rest or when long exposure times are required, I prefer Fujichrome 50 Velvia film. I am pleased with the film's color, its sharpness and its invisible grain. Fujichrome 100, Kodak Ektachrome Panther 100 and Fujichrome 50 are my choices for moving subjects, and rainy or overcast skies call for Kodachrome 200 film.

How to Photograph a Polar Bear

If you are trying to photograph a bear from a tundra buggy or a similar vehicle, a window seat is obviously in order. Frequently, the buggies are crowded, and only a monopod can be used to steady the camera. You may need to rest the lens on a small cushion, such as a beanbag, while taking the picture. Ask the driver to turn the temperature control of the vehicle's heating system as low as possible, because the warm air in the vehicle dissipates through the open windows and will waver in front of your lens, obscuring the clarity of your photograph. (This is a tip I picked up after developing dozens of rolls of film in which the images appeared out of focus. I subsequently noticed the warm air floating from the windows of adjacent vehicles.)

For professional photographers who do not want to get on board a buggy crammed with 35 passengers, there are three options: the three special vehicles operated by Don Walkosky, which are used by both tourists and professional photographers; the small bus operated by Churchill Wilderness Encounter; and a rented yellow Pro-Photo bus from Tundra Buggy.

Determining the correct exposure settings for a white polar bear on a white background is a challenge for even experienced professional photographers. When in doubt, use the "bracketing" method. Start by shooting at the suggested exposure setting, then take another shot at half an f-stop above and one at half an f-stop below the proposed setting. This will yield at least one correctly exposed picture. On a sunny day with reasonable snow cover, I use the override button and take my shots at +$1^{2}/_{3}$ f-stop above the suggested exposure setting.

What Is the Best Focal Length for Polar Bears?

There is no ideal lens for taking pictures of polar bears. A 20-600mm zoom would be ideal, but that will remain a dream for quite some time. Polar bears make an excellent subject for a 19mm wide-angle lens, which will show the bear in its impressive habitat. A 600mm lens is perfect for portraits of the white giants, and a 400mm f/2.8 is my favorite lens. If required, I use the 1.4x or 2x extender for 560mm or 800mm.

Setting Up the Shots in This Book

Note: Where more than one picture appears on a page, the following table will show more than one line of information for that page. The sequence will be for pictures from the top left to the bottom right.

Page	Camera	Lens	Setting
1	Leica R6	Summicron	2.0/50
2/3	Leica R6	Summicron	2.0/50
4/5	Leica R6.2	Apo Telyt	2.8/400
6	Leica R6	Apo Telyt	2.8/280
8	Leica R6.2	Apo Telyt	2.0/400
10	Leica R6.2	Apo Telyt	2.0/400
11	Leica R6	Summilux	1.4/80
13	Leica R6.2	Apo Telyt	2.0/400
14	Leica R7	Summicron	2.0/50
14	Leica R6.2	Summilux	1.4/80
14	Leica R6	Summilux	1.4/80
14	Leica R6	Summilux	1.4/80
15	Leica R6	Apo Telyt	2.8/280
16	Leica R6	Summilux	1.4/80
17	Leica R6.2	Apo Telyt	3.4/180
18	Leica R6.2	Apo Telyt	2.8/280
19	Leica R6.2	Apo Telyt	2.8/400
20	Canon F1	FD	4.0/200
21	Leica R6.2	Apo Telyt	2.0/400
22	Leica R6.2	Apo Telyt	2.0/400
23	Leica R6	Summilux	1.4/80
24/25	Canon F1	FD	4.5/500L
26	Leica R6	Apo Telyt	3.4/180
27	Leica R6	Apo Telyt	2.8/280
28	Leica R6.2	Apo Telyt	2.8/400
29	Leica R6.2	Apo Telyt	2.8/400
30	Leica R6	Apo Telyt	2.8/400
30	Leica R6	Apo Telyt	2.8/400
30	Leica R6	Apo Telyt	2.8/400
31	Leica R6	Apo Telyt	2.8/400
32	Leica R6.2	Apo Telyt	2.8/400
33	Leica R6.2	Apo Telyt	2.8/400
34	Leica R6.2	Apo Telyt	2.8/400
34	Leica R6.2	Apo Telyt	2.8/400
35	Leica R6.2	Apo Telyt	2.8/400
36	Leica R6.2	Apo Telyt	2.8/400
37	Leica R6.2	Apo Telyt	2.8/400
38	Leica R6.2	Summicron	2.0/50
39	Leica R6.2	Summicron	2.0/50
40	Leica R6.2	Apo Telyt	2.8/400
41	Leica R6	Apo Telyt	2.8/400
43	Leica R6	Apo Telyt	2.8/400
45	Leica R6	Apo Telyt	2.8/280
46	Leica R6.2	Apo Telyt	2.8/400
47	Leica R6	Apo Telyt	2.8/280
48	Leica R6	Apo Telyt	2.8/280
48	Leica R6	Apo Telyt	2.8/400
49	Leica R6	Apo Telyt	2.8/280
50	Leica R6	Apo Telyt	2.8/280
51	Leica R6.2	Apo Telyt	2.8/280
52/53	Leica R6	Apo Telyt	2.8/280
54	Leica R6.2	Apo Telyt	2.8/400
55	Leica R6.2	Apo Telyt	2.8/400
56	Leica R6.2	Summicron	2.0/50
56	Leica R6.2	Summicron	2.0/50
56/57	Leica R6.2	Summilux	1.4/35
57	Leica R6.2	Summicron	2.0/50
57	Leica R6.2	Summilux	1.4/80
58	Leica R6.2	Summilux	1.4/35
59	Leica R6.2	Apo Telyt	2.8/400
60/61	Leica R6.2	Summilux	1.4/35
62	Leica R6.2	Summilux	1.4/80
63	Leica R6.2	Elmarit	2.8/19
64	Leica R6.2	Summilux	1.4/35
64	Leica R6.2	Super Elmar	3.5/15
64	Leica R6	Summilux	1.4/80
65	Leica R6	Apo Telyt	2.8/280
66/67	Leica R6.2	Apo Telyt	2.8/400
68	Canon F1	FD	4.5/500L
69	Leica R6	Summilux	1.4/80
70	Canon F1	FD	4.5/500L
71	Leica R6	PC Super A.	2.8/28
72	Leica R6.2	Apo Telyt	2.8/400
73	Leica R6.2	Summilux	1.4/80
74	Leica R6	Summilux	1.4/80
75	Leica R6	Super Elmar	3.5/15
76	Leica R6.2	Elmarit	2.8/19
77	Leica R6	PC Super A.	2.8/28
78	Leica R6.2	Elmarit	2.8/19
79	Leica R6	A.M. Elmarit	2.8/100
80	Leica R6.2	Apo Telyt	2.8/400
81	Leica R6.2	Apo Telyt	2.8/400
82	Leica R6.2	Apo Telyt	2.8/400
83	Leica R6.2	Apo Telyt	2.8/400
83	Leica R6.2	Apo Telyt	2.8/400
84	Leica R6.2	Apo Telyt	2.8/400
85	Leica R6.2	Apo Telyt	2.8/400
86	Leica R6.2	Summicron	2.0/50
87	Leica R6.2	A.M. Elmarit	2.8/100
88	Canon F1	FD	4.5/500L
88	Leica R6	Apo Telyt	2.8/280
89	Leica R6	Elmarit	2.8/19
90	Leica R6	A.M. Elmarit	2.8/100
90	Leica R6	A.M. Elmarit	2.8/100
90	Leica R6	A.M. Elmarit	2.8/100
91	Canon F1	TS	2.8/35
92	Leica R6	Elmarit	2.8/19
92	Canon EOS1	EF	35/350
92	Leica R6	A.M. Elmarit	2.8/100
93	Leica R6.2	Summilux	1.4/80
94	Leica R7	Apo Telyt	2.8/400
94	Leica R7	Apo Telyt	2.8/400
95	Leica R7	Summicron	2.0/50
96	Leica R6.2	Apo Telyt	2.8/400
97	Leica R6.2	A.M. Elmarit	2.8/100
98	Leica R6.2	Apo Telyt	2.8/400
98	Leica R6.2	Apo Telyt	2.8/400
99	Leica R6.2	Apo Telyt	2.8/400
100	Leica R6.2	ApoTelyt	2.8/280
101	Leica R7	Apo Telyt	2.0/400
102	Canon EOS1	EF	4.5/500L
102	Canon EOS1	EF	4.5/500L
103	Canon EOSI	EF	4.5/500L
103	Canon EOS1	EF	4.5/500L
104	Canon EOS1	EF	4.5/500L
104	Canon EOS1	EF	4.5/500L
105	Canon EOS1	EF	4.5/500L
105	Canon EOS1	EF	4.5/500L
106	Leica R6	Apo Telyt	2.8/280
106	Leica R6	Apo Telyt	2.8/280
106	Leica R6	Apo Telyt	2.8/280
107	Canon EOS1	EF	4.5/500L
108	Leica R6	PC Super A.	2.8/28
109	Leica R6	Summilux	1.4/35
110	Leica R6	A.M. Elmarit	2.8/100
110	Leica R6	A.M. Elmarit	2.8/100
111	Leica R6	Apo Telyt	2.8/400
112	Leica R6	PC Super A.	2.8/28
113	Leica R6	Summilux	1.4/80
114	Canon F1	FD	4.5/500L
114	Canon F1	FD	4.5/500L
114	Canon F1	FD	4.5/500L
115	Leica R6	Summilux	1.4/35
117	Leica R6.2	Apo Telyt	3.4/180
118	Leica R6.2	Summicron	2.0/50
119	Leica R6.2	Summicron	2.0/50
120	Leica R6.2	Apo Telyt	2.8/280
121	Leica R6.2	Apo Telyt	2.8/280
122	Leica R6.2	Summicron	2.0/50
123	Leica R6	Apo Telyt	3.4/180
124	Leica R6.2	Summicron	2.0/50
125	Leica R6	Summilux	1.4/35
126	Leica R6.2	Apo Telyt	2.8/280
126	Leica R6.2	Apo Telyt	2.8/280
127	Leica R6.2	Apo Telyt	2.8/280
128	Leica R6	Apo Telyt	2.8/400
129	Leica R6	Apo Telyt	2.8/400
130	Leica R6.2	Apo Telyt	2.8/400
130	Leica R6.2	Apo Telyt	2.8/400
131	Leica R6.2	Apo Telyt	2.8/400
132	Leica R6.2	Apo Telyt	2.8/400
132	Leica R6.2	Apo Telyt	2.8/400
133	Leica R6.2	Apo Telyt	2.8/400
134	Leica R6.2	Summilux	1.4/80
135	Leica R6	Summilux	1.4/35
136	Leica R6.2	Summicron	2.0/50
137	Leica R6.2	Summilux	1.4/80
138	Leica R6	Summilux	1.4/35
138	Leica R6	Summicron	2.0/50
139	Leica R6	Apo Telyt	2.8/280
139	Leica R6	A.M. Elmarit	2.8/100
140	Leica R6	Summilux	1.4/80
140	Leica R6	Summilux	1.4/80
141	Leica R6.2	Apo Telyt	2.8/280
142	Leica R6	Summilux	1.4/80
142	Leica R6	Summilux	1.4/35
143	Leica R6	Summilux	1.4/80
145	Leica R6	Apo Telyt	2.8/280
146	Leica R6	Summilux	1.4/80
147	Leica R6	Summilux	1.4/35
147	Leica R6	Apo Telyt	2.8/280
148	Leica R6	Apo Telyt	2.8/280
149	Leica R6	Apo Telyt	2.8/280
150	Leica R6.2	Elmarit	2.8/19
151	Leica R6.2	Apo Telyt	2.8/400
153	Leica R6.2	Summilux	1.4/35
154	Leica R6.2	Summilux	1.4/35
155	Leica R6.2	Summilux	1.4/35
156/157	Leica R6.2	Summilux	1.4/35
158	Leica R6	Summilux	1.4/35
159	Leica R6	Summilux	1.4/35
160	Leica R6	Summilux	1.4/35
161	Leica R6	PC Super	A.2.8/28
162	Leica R6	Elmarit	2.8/19
163	Leica R6	Summilux	1.4/80
164	Leica R6.2	Super Elmar	3.5/15
165	Leica R6.2	Elmarit	2.8/19
167	Leica R6.2	Apo Telyt	2.8/400
168	Leica R6.2	Apo Telyt	2.8/400
169	Leica R6	Summicron	2.0/50
172	Leica R6	Summilux	1.4/35
175	Leica R6.2	Summilux	1.4/35

Capturing the Northern Lights

First of all, dress for the cold. Second, bring along an infinite supply of patience, a strong will and a healthy dose of determination—and, of course, your camera.

I use two manual cameras, since systems that require electrical energy will quickly shut down at temperatures below minus 22 degrees F. Before setting off in search of the northern lights, I remove the batteries. Fast lenses, such as the Summilux 1.4/35 or the Summilux 1.4/80, plus a sturdy tripod complement my equipment. In most cases, I use a Professional Manfrotto tripod or the Gitzo with Linhoff ball heads, since I frequently work with two cameras.

Film selection is somewhat more difficult. Fujichrome Velvia 50 might seem ideal, but it is too slow. Ektachrome 100 HC and Fujichrome 100 RDP are reasonable. However, they tend to break inside the camera at temperatures of minus 22 degrees F and below. Kodachrome 200 is more flexible and better tolerates the cold, but although it offers sufficient speed for the light show, exposures of $1/15$ second and longer produce reddish images. There are many 400, 800 and 1600 ASA films, but most feature a coarser grain structure and will not produce the desired results. That said, film selection remains a major challenge.

What about the surrounding light of the countryside? Is there any moonlight? Are there strong reflections from the snow? How bright are the northern lights themselves? The answers to these questions will lead to the correct camera settings. For general purposes, I recommend exposure times between 2 and 15 seconds. Many photographers have relied on their automatic light meters and have, in most instances, been left in the dark, because the cameras sensed unusable data.

Be careful not to exhale on the lens or the viewer or into the camera casing when changing the film. Vapor from your breath will immediately form small ice crystals that will scratch the film and obscure the lens. Also, only touch the camera and the wire release while wearing gloves; otherwise, they may freeze to your skin. (While setting up my camera one night, the wire release swung into my open mouth and instantly froze to my tongue. Removing the release was a painful experience.)

Most of the time, the wind blows from the bay at temperatures between minus 13 degrees F and minus 38 degrees. Under such conditions, it is of the utmost importance to check your skin regularly for signs of frostbite. This is when a photography buddy can come in handy. Frostbite yields a feeling of extreme coldness that turns to a hot sensation and finally leads to total numbness. The affected area then turns white.

The best locations for taking photographs of the northern lights are densely wooded areas or near wide, open lakes. Such locations are remote, isolated and absolutely still. February, March and April are the best times of the year to observe the northern lights. It is difficult to pinpoint the best hour of the night, so one must simply be on location and search the sky from about 6:00 in the evening to two hours after midnight. Auroras appear without warning and when you least expect them. Those who are willing to negotiate the aforementioned problems and who are fascinated by the phenomenon are in for the treat of a lifetime.

The Best Weeks for the Best Subjects

❊ **Northern Lights:** I recommend visiting from early March until mid-April. During this time, the weather is frequently cold but clear.

❊ **Snowdrifts:** Following the first blizzards in November until the last snowstorms in late April, there are always many opportunities to take pictures of snowdrifts. February and March offer ideal settings, especially right after one of the season's fierce storms.

❊ **Birds:** Geese begin to migrate in mid-May and can be observed until the first week in June. Terns appear by the thousands during the first two weeks in June, when the ice on the rivers starts to break up. In general, June is the time for bird migration, and many birds start to breed in the area. It is the best time of the year to observe the rare Ross' gulls and the northern hawk owls in the ponds near Churchill. The young hawk owls and great gray owls hatch in mid-June.

❊ **Whales:** The first belugas show up in early June, but the main whale season is from mid-July until late August, when up to 3,000 whales appear each day.

❊ **Foxes:** Arctic foxes are visible at their dens from the end of June.

❊ **Colors:** Autumn colors begin to emerge in the third week in August.

❊ *Ursus maritimus:* The official polar bear season starts October 10 and ends sometime between October 25 and November 3.

Bibliography

Wildflowers of Churchill and the Hudson Bay Region, Karen L. Johnston, photography Robert Taylor, 1987.

Handbook of Snow, Pergamon Press, Hammerweg 6, Kronberg/Taunus, Germany.

The Aurora Watcher's Handbook, Neil Davis, University of Alaska Press, Fairbanks, 1992.

Aurora Borealis, The Amazing Northern Light, S.-I. Akasofu, Alaska Geographic Society, 1979.

Rainbows, Halos, and Glories, Robert Greenler, Cambridge University Press, 1980.

Churchill: Polar Bear Capital of the World, Mark Fleming, Hyperion Press Ltd., 1988.

World of the Polar Bears, Fred Bruemmer, Key Porter Books, 1989.

Polar Bears, Ian Stirling, photography Dan Guravich, Fitzhenry & Whiteside Ltd., Markham, Ontario, 1988.

The Cubs' World, Richard Perry, Cassell & Comp. Ltd., London, 1966.

"The Polar Bear Control Program at Churchill, Manitoba," Stephen R. Kearney, Wildlife Branch, Natural Resources, Thompson, Manitoba.

GEO Magazin, Nr. 2/91, Germany "Der Bär ist gut in Schuß."

"Changing Atmosphere," published by Authority of the Minister of Environment 1989, Sterne and Weltraum, 6/89, Juni, 28. Jahrgang, Dr. Vehrenberg GmbH, 8000 München 90, Germany.

Kosmos Magazin, Nr. 12/92, Germany, text by Dr. Köthe, photography Norbert Rosing.

Kosmos Magazin, Nr. 12/91, Germany, Dickes Fell and Kalte Füße.

BBC Wildlife, Vol. 11, Number 2, February 1993, Pol Star.

"The Great White Bears," Robert W. Nero, Province of Manitoba, 8/1989.

Wildlife Conservation, 7/8/93.

Churchill as a Tourist Town

There are five hotels in Churchill, ranging from low-budget to standard ratings. A number of restaurants offer everything from gourmet food and home-cooked meals to fast food. Edgar's Place is within the Town Complex. Here, locals exchange the latest news and gossip. Churchill has only one bakery, and those who prefer to prepare their own food will find all the essentials in one of the two supermarkets. The post office, telephone office, train station and banks operate during normal business hours. Souvenirs are available from a large selection of places, such as the Arctic Trading Post or Northern Images. The Eskimo Museum, the biggest of its kind in northern Canada, is worth a visit. The library in Churchill's Town Complex is another source for books and magazines on the Arctic. A private picture gallery plus free video presentations on polar bears enhance the spare-time activities of the town. The Town Complex also has workout facilities, an indoor swimming pool, a bowling alley and a sports arena that allow visitors to relax and revive themselves at the end of a long tour through the arctic region.